Dedic

To my wife, Martha, who h
for more than

TEXAS UNEXPLAINED

Contents

Introduction	vii
How Do I Know a Ghost If I See One?	1
Resurrection of Buck Creek	9
Konate's Staff	15
True Believer	25
The Stone Heads of Malakoff	35
Interview with Cheetwah	43
The Mystery of the Lady in Blue	53
The Strange Odyssey of the Good Ship *Lively*	69
The Spirits of Goliad	77
The Truth About Sasquatch	95
Humming with the Hummers	107
That Night at the Vaudeville	115
Major Sources	129

Introduction

I had a lot of trouble with my Muse as I wrote this collection of stories about the unexplained side of Texas. We bickered over everything from grammar to punctuation to spelling to story treatment. We did agree on the book's purpose, which is to share with you some of the state's surprisingly rich legacy of mysteries, but we argued over nearly everything else.

As it turned out, when my Muse was reasonably sober, I produced some perfectly straightforward stories. When he had been tippling, though, I spun out some less-than-serious stuff just to keep the peace. Once, when he was dreadfully hung over, he left me alone and I wrote one of the pieces all by myself. It is based on an experience my grandmother, a Texas pioneer, had in the Panhandle more than forty years ago.

If the stories are different one from the other, depending on the condition of my Muse, they do share a common theme of mystery. In the following pages, you will find ghosts, spirits, apparitions, eerie sounds, uncanny natural events, spiritual experiences, visions, strange lights, baffling discoveries, buried treasure, a lost ship, inexplicable sounds, a monster, a natural miracle, and an enigmatic assassination. You will also learn about places in Texas you can visit where you might experience some of the mysteries firsthand.

Meanwhile, I will probably look for a new Muse, but I suppose that I am stuck with the one I have. At least I do not have to share any royalties with him.

How Do I Know a Ghost If I See One?

ASHTON VILLA

"Ashton Villa does look elegant and proud, don't you think so, sir?"

The golden-haired young woman, perhaps five and a half feet tall, scarcely more than a girl, spoke to me in the rich, modulated, lyrical voice of the South.

I had started at the discovery of her standing there next to me, beside the wrought-iron front gate with its cornstalk posts. It was as though she had materialized out of the warm, humid air of that late-afternoon summer day at Galveston Island. Somehow she seemed as cool as the shaded north slope of an Alpine meadow at sunset. I could almost feel the chill. I shivered. She reminded me of Renoir's ethereal portrayals of young French women late in the nineteenth century. She wore a long white dress trimmed with elegant lace. It appeared as diaphanous as the wisp of a cloud. She seemed as delicate as a butterfly, yet somehow assertive, self-assured, her eyes intense and searching.

I had paused on the sidewalk in front of Ashton Villa after a long walk to study and think about the three-story Italianate-style antebellum mansion that James Moreau Brown had built of brick and decorated with filigreed ironwork in Galveston in 1859. It was the first of the great Victorian residences to be constructed on Broadway, the famed old boulevard that conducts you from the mainland into the city. On the front lawn towering palm trees swayed with gentle grace.

"Sometimes I come here just to admire her," said the young woman. "Her very walls resonate with history. She served as a hospital during the War, you know."

"Which war?" I asked.

"Why, sir, the War for Southern Independence, what some called the Civil War," she said. "Generals from both armies used Ashton Villa as their headquarters. Not at the same time, of course." She smiled at her own humor.

"Swords of surrender changed hands in the living room . . . the Gold Room, it is called. It's a perfectly splendid room located there on the first floor, the corner on your left." I could sense the nostalgia in her voice, a kind of longing that seemed strange for a woman so young.

"After the War, the famous and the wealthy came to the parties and the dinners and the balls at Ashton Villa. There was such gaiety. Have you been inside, sir?"

"Not yet," I said. "My wife and I plan to visit the house tomorrow."

"You will enjoy it. It's open for tours almost every day."

"I have read that Ashton Villa is haunted."

" 'Haunted' is such an ugly word," she said. "The spirit of Miss Bettie, Mr. Brown's daughter, has graced Ashton Villa since her untimely death in 1920. She couldn't bear the thought of leaving.

"People said Miss Bettie had a radiant beauty." The young woman reached in her purse for a mirror. She carefully studied the reflection of her face, her golden hair spiraled gracefully atop her head. She seemed pleased with what she saw.

"Miss Bettie had many admirers. She dressed like a princess. She hosted the affairs for her father at Ashton Villa. She played the piano beautifully. She studied art in Europe. She traveled across the Continent and collected marvelous things—paintings . . . tapestries . . . fans. She treasured exquisite fans, fans of peacock feathers, fans from the Orient. She never married. She loved her freedom too much."

"You seem to know a lot about Ashton Villa and Miss Bettie," I said.

"Oh, I do," she said. "Sir, do you believe in spirits?"

"Ghosts?"

"All right, ghosts."

"I wouldn't know a ghost if I saw one."

"Sometimes . . . " the young woman said slowly, as if she were sorting through remembrances and feelings, "you just know that something—a presence!—is there. You can sense it. You can feel it. You feel . . . a certain cold in the air. Sometimes you hear footsteps."

I shivered slightly. I felt as if a fresh breeze had arisen from the waters of the Gulf and put its feathery arms around me. The lengthening shadows of the lofty palm trees lay across Ashton Villa's lawn.

"Sometimes, of course, you actually see spirits, or ghosts. As if they were real, living people. Flesh and bone and blood. But, more likely, a kind of vaporous figure, floating like a wisp of smoke. Occasionally, ghosts may announce their presence with an ephemeral sort of light.

"Ghosts are never ordinary-looking. The women may be very beautiful or frightfully ugly, the men quite handsome or maybe fearsome in appearance. Children always have big, innocent eyes and smooth, almost translucent skin. The old show the wear of their years—terribly wrinkled skins, stooped backs, slow and careful movement. Most often, spirits dress in pure white or black, just occasionally in other colors.

"Sometimes a ghost sings—soft, melancholy songs. A ghost may play a piano or an organ or a harp or a flute or a violin. A ghost may ring bells like those in a church tower—muted, very softly, you understand. You hear the music or the chimes, rising and falling softly, sometimes fading away, as if the sound were carried to you from a great distance by a restless and gentle wind of uncertain origin. You seldom know quite where it comes from. Lovely, if you listen well."

"I have never seen a ghost," I said.

"You often find them near places they loved when they were living persons," said the young woman. "Like Miss Bettie, who so loved Ashton Villa." She again examined the reflection of her face in her mirror. She brushed back one of her golden curls, that had wandered from its appointed place. Again she looked pleased.

"You may find ghosts searching eternally, usually in the depth of night, at those places where they lost people they loved," she continued. "Mothers search for their children. Lovers search for each other. You may find ghosts at places where they lost their own lives, frequently in some kind of tragedy. You may find them wandering like lost souls along lonely roads, isolated beaches, swamps, or forests. You will naturally find ghosts in cemeteries or at graves where their bodies were entombed, or sometimes even near secret sites where treasures were hidden.

"You find them at summer twilight, especially when there is a full moon, or during thunderstorms, or on foggy evenings.

"Sometimes apparitions appear with ghosts. Phantom images of ships at sea, a racing white stallion across a grassy plain, aircraft from the great world wars, headstones in a far distant churchyard."

"That sounds spooky to me," I said.

"I suppose it is," said the young woman, "but many ghosts bring a special delight to a place. Miss Bettie . . . still lights up Ashton Villa. She still captivates visitors. People still come here for parties and weddings and celebrations. Yet . . . there are some . . ."

I felt the chill again. The young woman had fallen silent.

"Some what?" I prompted her.

"Some . . . ghosts . . . who are not so nice. Some frighten the living, their animals, even other ghosts right out of their wits."

"I have read about some of those," I said. " Washington Irving wrote about a headless ghost—a Hessian whose head was separated from his body by a cannonball—who rode a great black steed and wore a cloak and scared Ichabod Crane into the next century." I warmed at the recollection of the wonderful old story, "The Legend of Sleepy Hollow."

"Texas has its own headless ghosts," the young woman said quite seriously. "Lots of them. Up in Dickens County, on the old McKenzie Trail, the headless ghost of Burt—I don't know his last name—still lurks around the ruins of the old dugout where his partner, Ben, chopped his head off with an ax. Both were squatters.

"In Panna Maria, that little town southeast of San Antonio, a headless figure in a black cloak searches for his skull, lost when his bones and those of others were being re-interred to make way for the construction of a church.

"West of Corpus Christi, a headless man rides a magnificent charging gray stallion in the night at a place called Dead Man's Lagoon, the scene where the poor fellow won a high-stakes horse race but lost his head to the machetes of those he left in his dust.

"The Presidio la Bahía at Goliad has a headless horseman too. Fort Leaton at Presidio has a headless horseman who wears a black cape and rides a white horse. We have these and a lot of other headless ghosts in Texas.

"Some ghosts, vile creatures, behave so badly that they embarrass all the other ghosts. They frighten the living needlessly. They try to lure innocent people into danger. They play tricks. They break things. They steal things. They cause terrible accidents. They take great glee in the bad things they do," the young woman concluded.

"I've read about some of those ghosts," I said.

The young woman resumed, "An old squatter's ghost used to drive his phantom steers into herds that cowboys were holding for the night on a high bluff at the eastern edge of the Caprock, in Crosby County. The place isn't far from the river bottom where Coronado camped during his Spanish expedition across the Texas Panhandle in 1541, searching for cities of gold.

"The old squatter's ghost and his phantom animals spooked the herds and stampeded them over the bluff. He killed hundreds of head of livestock over the years, and he killed and hurt several cowboys. The ghost had returned for revenge after a trail boss murdered the squatter in 1889 by forcing him and his blindfolded horse over the bluff.

"One cowboy, riding night guard with a herd, saw the squatter's ghost. 'It looked like a man on a horse, but it just seemed to float along,' he said. Ghost steers seemed to sail in the darkness 'through the herd and right past your horse.' It was 'scary.'

"Stampede Mesa, they call the place now. It got so bad that cattlemen wouldn't dare try to hold their herds up on that bluff anymore."

I replied, "You can scarcely blame some ghosts for what they do after what happened to them in life."

This young woman of the South looked pained and thoughtful, as though she recalled a dark secret.

"The ghosts of some sixty slaves, buried in a forgotten cemetery near Lake Houston in Montgomery County, have taken a terrible toll on people living in houses built unknowingly over their graves. The neighborhood is called Newport. The ghosts have caused lights to switch on and off in homes, sudden powerful winds to whip through doors and windows, sinkholes to appear in the earth. They have caused an unusually high number of terrible illnesses. They caused a young woman to die of a heart attack after she warned her mother not to dig in the family backyard. They caused the young woman's sister to go mad. Many people moved away from Newport to escape the ghosts of the slaves."

"You have a broad knowledge of ghosts," I said, "especially for a person so young."

"I've been interested in ghosts for a long time," she said, smiling slightly, as though recalling an ironic and personal secret. "Sometimes ghosts do neither harm nor good. They just remind us of past horrifying events.

"The spirit of Chipita Rodriguez still appears from the mists of night in the coastal river bottoms of San Patricio County, recalling the day in 1863 when she was hanged for a crime that she denied ever committing.

"A jury had found Chipita, a tiny, frail woman, guilty of attacking John Savage, a large, powerful man who was a horse trader, splitting his head, and dismembering his body with an ax. She robbed him of six hundred dollars, they believed. The judge sentenced her to hang.

"As she prepared to die on that November day, two sisters, Rachel and Eliza Sullivan, who believed in her innocence, bathed and dressed her. They combed and braided her long hair.

"Her executioners hammered together a crude wooden coffin and loaded it onto a wagon. They took Chipita from the jail and forced her to sit on her own coffin as they transported her to the hanging tree, a large mesquite near a riverbank. There she could see the freshly dug grave that awaited her body.

"She stood in the back of the wagon as the hangman placed a noose about her delicate neck. She refused the offer of a blindfold. She whispered to the hangman, *'Libre de culpa'* (not guilty). She smoked a last cigarette.

"Deputy John Gilpin drove the team and wagon forward, out from under Chipita, leaving her dangling from the rope, her unmasked face contorted, her body flailing in agony. Her elfin figure lacked the weight that would cause her neck to snap. Eventually, though, her body stilled. Gilpin decided that Chipita must have suffocated and died. He ordered her body released from the noose and buried.

"His men placed Chipita in the crude coffin and lowered it into the grave. They began covering her with dirt. A bystander heard a moan, then pounding, from inside the coffin. He fled.

"Gilpin's men covered the coffin and filled in the grave as Chipita Rodriguez's moans and pounding faded into silence beneath the earth.

"Later someone found John Savage's six hundred dollars still in his saddlebags. There had been no robbery."

The young woman stood silent there before Ashton Villa for a long moment. "If I had been Chipita Rodriguez," I ventured, "I would haunt someone, too."

"I know of evil ghosts," said the young woman. "I know of ghosts who remind us of the anguish of their deaths. I also know of ghosts who mirror the kindness embedded in the human soul.

"The spirit of a feeble old woman clothed in the dress of one of Mexico's ancient Indian civilizations has saved the lives of many in the lands around Brownsville, at the far southern tip of Texas. She is so beloved that the people call her '*abuela*,' or 'grandmother.'

"Many years ago, she rescued a child, four-year-old Consuelo, who had been lost in the mesquite brush for five days. Consuelo had wandered off while her impoverished parents, the Garzas, labored in the fields just outside of Brownsville. The old woman delivered the child to her home, safe and sound, then vanished before the ecstatic parents could even say thank you. Throughout her life, Consuelo remembered the experience and her *abuela*.

"Another time, the old woman, in her ancient native dress, appeared at a desolate farm hut to minister to a young mother in labor. The husband had rushed frantically into the nearest town for a midwife, leaving his wife temporarily alone and terrified, struggling to bring a new life into the world. The old woman appeared as if in response to a prayer, and she cared for the mother, delivered her baby, cleansed them both, and nestled the baby in its mother's arms. When the husband and midwife arrived, they found mother and child sleeping peacefully. The old woman had vanished before anyone could say 'thank you,' but the young couple took her into their hearts and memories as their special *abuela*.

"The ghosts of old people are not the only ones who care about the living. On the south side of San Antonio, at a railroad crossing near the San Juan Capistrano Mission, the ghosts of children who were killed in a terrible train and school bus collision back in the 1940's push vehicles clear of the tracks to prevent other accidents. They even leave their fingerprints on the fenders and bumpers of the cars."

The sun rested on the western horizon now, the last shafts of the day's light falling on Ashton Villa's front porch. "Of all the ghosts you know," I asked the young woman, "who is your favorite?"

She thought for a long moment. She pulled the mirror from her purse and studied her face. "Miss Bettie Brown," she said, almost sadly, it seemed.

"Of Ashton Villa. Right here. Those who see her spirit find her as enchantingly beautiful as ever." She returned her mirror to its home in her purse. "The ghosts of old beaux still come to see her when night falls. She plays the marvelous old square grand piano in the Gold Room, which she decorated herself. It's a work of art. She still cherishes the treasures she collected in Europe those many years ago. She relishes her paintings, which hang on the walls. She loves the gaiety, the company, the music of the festivities that people still hold at Ashton Villa."

With darkness falling, I noticed that a soft golden light had appeared in the first-floor windows of the corner of the house, the location of the Gold Room. I knew that gas-lighted chandeliers must hang from the ceiling.

"I must go now," said the young woman, and she abruptly opened the iron gate of Ashton Villa's front-yard fence and walked up the sidewalk, onto the porch, and through the front door. She almost seemed to vanish into the old house.

It occurred to me that I had forgotten to ask the young woman her name.

A late-evening herring gull soared above me, screaming, and headed for the beach.

I turned away from Ashton Villa and started down Broadway, past a large and beautiful flower garden and gazebo, and into the twilight. I thought I could hear a piano playing softly, the melody carried on the wind.

Perhaps my wife and I would see the young woman tomorrow when we visited Ashton Villa. We would ask her name then.

Resurrection of Buck Creek

"Buck Creek has dried up," my grandmother, Minnie Woodley, said. I could see the despair in her eyes. I had come home from Austin for the summer after my first year at the University of Texas.

In normal times, Buck Creek rose in a marsh in a pasture on the western edge of my grandmother's land, which was located in Cottle County, about ten miles south of Paducah, and flowed lazily eastward, through a Bermuda grass meadow just south of her house, beneath willow and cottonwood trees, forming occasional murky pools. It was one of the very few live freshwater streams in the southeastern corner of the Texas Panhandle.

"Has it ever dried up before?" I asked.

"Not since I've lived on the land, and I've been there for nearly fifty years."

I remembered fishing in Buck Creek's dark pools for catfish and sunfish. I used a cane pole rigged with string, a small hook, lead shot, and a bottle-cork bobber. I used a sharp knife to split the bottle cork half-way, then forced the string into the split to the center. I could then slide the cork up and down on the string to adjust the fishing depth of the hook. For bait, I dug earthworms behind one of my grandmother's sheds. I caught my first fish out of Buck Creek when I was six or seven years old.

I remembered lying on the bank of the creek in the shade of the trees on still, hot summer days. Through the branches above my head, I watched turkey vultures, soaring elegantly in the updrafts rising from the hot earth. I listened to the melancholy, flutelike call of the mourning doves and to the optimistic and prissy call of the bobwhite quail.

I remembered the night that my father fried a fresh catch of Buck Creek's fish on the wood-fired cookstove in my grandmother's kitchen and made "fish gravy" from a mixture of cornmeal and the grease. In those days, her home was still illuminated by coal oil lamps, which threw off a soft warm yellow light and a slightly pungent smell. It was the best meal I ever ate.

I remembered riding a gentle paint horse named Pet along Buck Creek, her shod hooves clattering on the cobbles when we crossed the stream, and I remembered the smells of her sweat and the saddle leather on hot summer afternoons.

I remembered sleeping outdoors in the summers, on the porch at my grandmother's house, where I could hear the sounds of the night. Howls rolled up the slope from the creek and faded away into the darkness. "Coyotes," my grandfather said to me from his bed, knowing I needed reassurance. I listened to the howls for some time, then I could hear a pair of coyotes yipping as they hunted together along the creek in the darkness. I could hear the bullfrogs on the creek, their bellows so deep and rumbling you could almost feel the vibrations in the air. I could hear other sounds, too, which I couldn't identify. Sometimes I could hear nothing. Silence.

What I recalled most vividly about Buck Creek, though, was the marsh that surrounded the spring. I remembered it as a brooding, primeval place of deep shade, mystery, and magic. I watched the fluttering red-winged blackbirds that lived among the cattail reeds at the edge of the marsh. I watched a blotchy dark brown water snake swallow a fish, caught at the edge of the pool that marked the emergence of the spring. I watched a great horned owl fly through the trees and the shadows in absolute silence, like an apparition, disappearing, and I felt as if I had awakened from a dream.

I knew from my grandfather that there was a grave near the marsh, where a seasonal laborer from Mexico and his wife had buried their baby, who died suddenly from illness or injury years before I was born. There had been no doctor to help the child, no priest to administer last rites. The man and his wife packed their things and went back to Mexico. They never returned. I searched for the grave, looking for the remains of a cross, a mound of earth, a pile of stones, but the site where they buried their baby had vanished.

I remembered Buck Creek in a certain way, locked in my mind like a book of images and experiences that I didn't want to give up. My grandmother knew that when she told me that the stream had dried up. Whatever I wanted, times were changing.

The year was 1955, the sixth straight year of one of the most prolonged and searing droughts in Texas history, which would last a seventh year, reaching biblical proportions, like Egypt's seven years of dearth in the book of Genesis.

The southwest wind, powered by the summer heat, blew so incessantly that elm and mulberry trees all developed a permanent northeastward lean, as if they were trying to flee. The wind picked up the dust and sand from powder-dry fields and overgrazed pastures, raised clouds of dirt into the sky, and redeposited it in the fields, leveling plowed furrows and blanketing and smothering young cotton, maize, and corn. It piled sand against the southwestern sides of houses and even on porches and in garages. It pushed sand dunes over barbed-wire fences and across highways.

"The dust, the dust, the beautiful dust / On the evil and the just!" wrote an embittered anonymous author in the local paper. "From the North and from the South / In the eyes, the nose, the mouth / On the shrubs, the flowers, the trees / On the fence, the gate, the shed / On the table and the bed / On the window, on the door / In the floor / On the gallop, on the run, on the stairway to the sun / On the ladder to the moon, on the wings at night, at noon, on the street and on the square / The dust, the dust is everywhere! / The dust, the beautiful dust!"

In the summer of 1953 the farmers of Cottle County held an all-night prayer for rain, and they were rewarded with two inches on July 16. It wasn't nearly enough.

In April 1954, a strange and frightening black cloud appeared across the northern horizon about midmorning on a day that had dawned perfectly clear, still, and promising. By noon, the cloud, drifting dust that had risen from plains to the north, covered the land like a shroud. The sun disappeared. Total blackness descended, like the closing of a vault.

From 1950 through 1956, crops failed. Farmers sold out. Families abandoned homes to the winds and the sands, leaving places where they had lived for generations. An infestation of flies triggered an outbreak of polio. Young people graduated and left for war, bigger cities, job opportunities, new lives. Few stayed in Cottle County.

The hardships weighed heavily on my grandmother, too. She lost her husband, my grandfather, who died after a long illness in 1952. She saw her two sons, my uncles, leave Cottle County to search for work in Los Angeles and Lubbock. They had to support their families. She was left to face the drought alone, a woman in her sixties, with a thousand acres of unirrigated cropland and pasture and more than a hundred head of livestock.

She could have sold out and left. Many did. It never crossed her mind.

She worked her fields herself. She plowed the soil. She planted and cultivated her cotton and maize. She maintained her tractor and its implements. She fed her livestock, doctored her baby calves. She kept up her home, her barn, her corrals. She worked beside the men she hired to help with the harvests when crops did make. She paid her bills. She endured.

Occasionally, on a Sunday afternoon, she saddled her favorite horse and rode for pleasure along the gently flowing waters of Buck Creek. The never-failing spring became for her a renewal of soul, a reaffirmation of the human spirit, an enduring source of hope. "There was nothing I ever did that I enjoyed more," she told me.

But in the summer of 1955, the sixth year of that terrible drought, the Buck Creek spring had failed, and the gently flowing waters stilled and began to evaporate into the blistering summer sky. Catfish and sunfish congregated as solid, writhing masses in dwindling stagnant black puddles, gasping desperately, the sun burning their exposed backs. Then the water was gone. The creek bottom turned into a desiccated black powder.

My grandmother stopped riding along the creek on Sunday afternoons.

A year later, in the summer of 1956, I returned to the southeastern Panhandle from my second year at the University of Texas, to the winds, the airborne dust, deserted farm homes, failing crops, barren pastures, closed and shuttered businesses, dwindling population. The nearer I got to home, the more my spirits fell. I knew then that I would never come back here to live. I thought that all the things I valued must be gone forever.

When I saw my grandmother, though, she said, "Buck Creek is flowing again." I could see that her despair from the year before had lifted.

"But there hasn't been any rain," I said. "Where could it have gotten the water? How can it be flowing?"

"It's flowing," she insisted. "It happened a few weeks ago. I was feeling so blue—I thought I would have to sell all my cows. I didn't have enough water for them. I just didn't know what I was going to do."

She had come to her house in the late afternoon after a day in her fields under a heavy sun. For the first time in months she felt strangely drawn to the creek, to where the spring had risen in the marsh. She walked down the slope from her house through a trail in the Bermuda grass to the bank of the creek and turned upstream toward the marsh. The red-winged blackbirds, the brown water snakes, the great horned owls, the catfish, the sunfish, the bullfrogs, the coyotes, all but the lost grave of a forgotten Mexican child, were gone, but she found the old quietness, some of the mystery and magic, in the lengthening shadows of willow and cottonwood trees.

"I thought I'd walk up to where the spring used to be. I don't know why," she said. "I just felt drawn. Then I saw the water coming down the creek bed to meet me. It was moving slow, just a trickle. At first, I couldn't believe it. I walked up to the spring, and the pool where it rose was full again. Buck Creek had returned to life before my eyes. It was running again. I knew then that things were going to be all right."

The following year, 1957, the drought broke. The rains returned. My grandmother continued to farm her land and raise her cows for another three decades. She lived in the house on Buck Creek, the home she moved into when she married at sixteen, the home where she had borne and raised four children and spoiled seven grandchildren, until January 10, 1990, when she was ninety-six and her heart simply ceased to beat.

As far as I know, Buck Creek has never gone dry again.

KONATE'S STAFF

WOLF ENCOUNTER
HUECO TANKS

From the sheltering mouth of their cave, which now seemed more like a tomb than a defensive refuge, some twenty Kiowa raiders watched the fires of the Mexican militia appear one after the other on the darkening rocky desert hillsides of the natural amphitheater. One flared up to illuminate and expose the only water hole, which might otherwise have been approachable under the cover of darkness.

The Kiowas heard the mechanical rattle of firearms, the thud of boots, the Spanish speech and taunting laughter of the soldiers, the occasional whinnying of the military horses, the day's last shrill and mocking cries of red-tailed hawks soaring in the freedom of the skies.

They smelled the stench of death: the decaying flesh of their horses, gunned down by the soldiers; the putrefying wounds of Dagoi, shot by the soldiers as he attempted to reach water; the bloated corpse of one of their comrades, mortally wounded on the first day of the siege that the Kiowas now endured at the hands of the Mexican troops.

They tasted the maddening dryness of thirst in the mouth and throat and suffered the incessant gnawing of hunger in the belly. They tried to lick water from the damp surfaces of the cave's stone walls. They tried to eat the rotting flesh of their dead horses. It only added to their torment.

They felt the darkness closing over them like a shroud in this dimly lit primeval chamber, its moonscape of dark jumbled stone forged in the molten heart of the earth.

The siege, in the summer of 1839, had begun nine days earlier, when the militia struck the Kiowas in the amphitheater in the heart of the West Texas hills of Hueco Tanks. Hundreds of miles from home, the Kiowas, who had called off a planned raid on El Paso, were aware that no one from their tribe knew of their plight nor of the need to rescue them. They stood alone, cut off, beyond help.

Konate was a warrior who could not foresee the experience that lay just ahead and that would fuse him with Kiowa legend. Like the other raiders, he yearned to return home . . . home! . . . to the high plains of the Texas Panhandle and the rolling red plains to the east.

Konate wondered if he would ever again see the southwest wind ripple the vast sea of buffalo and grama grasses on the plains; the great herds of buffalo—as important to the Kiowa as air to the lungs—as they migrated by the millions in their seasonal processions across the Llano Estacado; the bands of antelope as they fled before Kiowa horses in an uncanny orchestrated ballet of fleetness and grace; the flocks of ducks and geese as they rose like leaves in a giant whirlwind from the buffalo wallows and playa lakes on a gray and cold winter day; the gaillardia that spread like washes of red and gold paint from the feet to the horizon as the spring sun warmed the earth.

He wondered if he would ever again hear the rattling gobble of wild turkeys; the piercing low-high fluted notes of the bobwhite quail; the scream of soaring golden eagles; the alternating yelps of hunting coyote; or—that most haunting of all sounds—the howls of gray wolves on moonlit nights on the high plains.

He wondered if he would ever again smell buckskins soaked in the sweat of his hard-run pony or buffalo meat roasting over a campfire fueled by the wood of a pecan tree or the aromatic smoke of kinnikinnick rising from the pipes of the old men lazing in the sun.

Like the other raiders, trapped and desperate in the blackness of the Hueco Tanks cave, Konate wondered if he would ever again experience the tribal Sun Dance, that magical early-summer moment of annual renewal for the Kiowas, the festive spiritual pinnacle of their year.

He knew that the tribe would celebrate next year's Sun Dance in the northern Panhandle's Canadian River brakes, where the river receives the waters of Mustang Creek. He could visualize the coming together of the tribal bands, the rekindling of friendships, the great circular encampment of tepees, the festiveness of the days, the feasts of buffalo meat, the joining of young women and warriors, the deeply ceremonial and joyous raising of the medicine lodge, the offering of the sacrificial buffalo hide, the dancing of warriors to the throb of drums and the trilling of eagle-bone flutes.

In his mind's eye, Konate could see the Sun Dance chief take his place at the western side of the medicine lodge. He could see the annual unveiling and display of the Tai-me, an icon of the Kiowas' powerful and beneficent god and the spiritual centerpiece of the Sun Dance. Fashioned from a dark green stone shaped like a human head and adorned with ermine, feathers, and blue beads, the traditional Tai-me icon, no more than two feet in length, evoked a profound sense of holiness for Kiowas in the medicine lodge, similar to the sense of spirituality that the icon of a patron saint brings to the faithful in a Catholic cathedral.

Together, the Sun Dance and the Tai-me symbolized the new season's resurrection of the earth and the renewal of the tribal soul.

The yearning for home and family and tribe magnified the desperation of the raiders, imprisoned in their dark cave at Hueco Tanks.

Earlier in the siege, the Kiowas had thought they had discovered a possible escape route, an ascending seventy-foot-high shaft at the end of a long passageway. Piercing the darkness at the top of the shaft, a fleck of the blue of the daylight sky was just visible. Laboriously, they moved dirt and stone debris from the shaft. They managed to enlarge the opening just enough to writhe through to the surface for a possible bolt to freedom. They could see an escape route that the soldiers apparently did not watch.

But before the Kiowas could make their break, the Mexicans discovered the opening, promptly pouring stone and earth into it to reseal it.

Hope turned to despair.

They could see other openings in the roof of the cave, but a climb up precipitous stone to these openings looked treacherous, all but impossible. Besides, the soldiers had surely posted watches at these potential escape routes.

As the siege wore on, one of the soldiers' Indian scouts stood on a ridge above the cave and called down to the raiders, speaking in the language of the Comanches, who were Kiowa allies in the Texas Panhandle and western Oklahoma. "Don't give up," the scout cried. "The Mexicans are going to throw some food down to you soon. It will be all right, because they want to take you alive."

Despair turned to hope.

The raiders heard something thud to the floor of the amphitheater, at the front of their cave. Driven by thirst and hunger, they rushed out, only to be met by gunfire and the "food," which they discovered to be . . . rattlesnakes. They scrambled frantically to avoid the venomous fangs and kill the snakes, all the while hearing the derisive laughter of their tormentors in the hills above.

Hope turned to despair.

The tenth day of the siege. Despondency. Hopelessness.

Finally, one of the Kiowa warriors,

Tsone-ai-tah, said to his comrades. "We are going to die here like helpless women." The raiders raised their heads and fixed their eyes on Tsone-ai-tah. "If you are willing to die like women, there is no help for us," he said. "Let us get out of this foul place and die in the open like men and warriors!"

His words galvanized the Kiowas. They decided that when night fell, they would make a desperate attempt to ascend to one of the perilous openings and break for their freedom. They would not—could not—stop for anyone who might fall to a Mexican bullet. That could mean death for them all.

Dohasan, the renowned principal chief of the Kiowas, took command, even though he had joined the raiding party only as a participant, not as the leader. The raiders stripped leather thongs from their leggings to make ropes for the climb. They tied their bows to their wrists so they could retrieve the weapons should they be dropped during the climb out.

At last they stood ready.

Dagoi, the warrior who had lain wounded throughout the siege, begged the warriors to take him with them. "I want to see my father's face again," he said.

"It is our life or yours," Dohasan told him grimly. "Make your heart strong. Die like a Kiowa warrior."

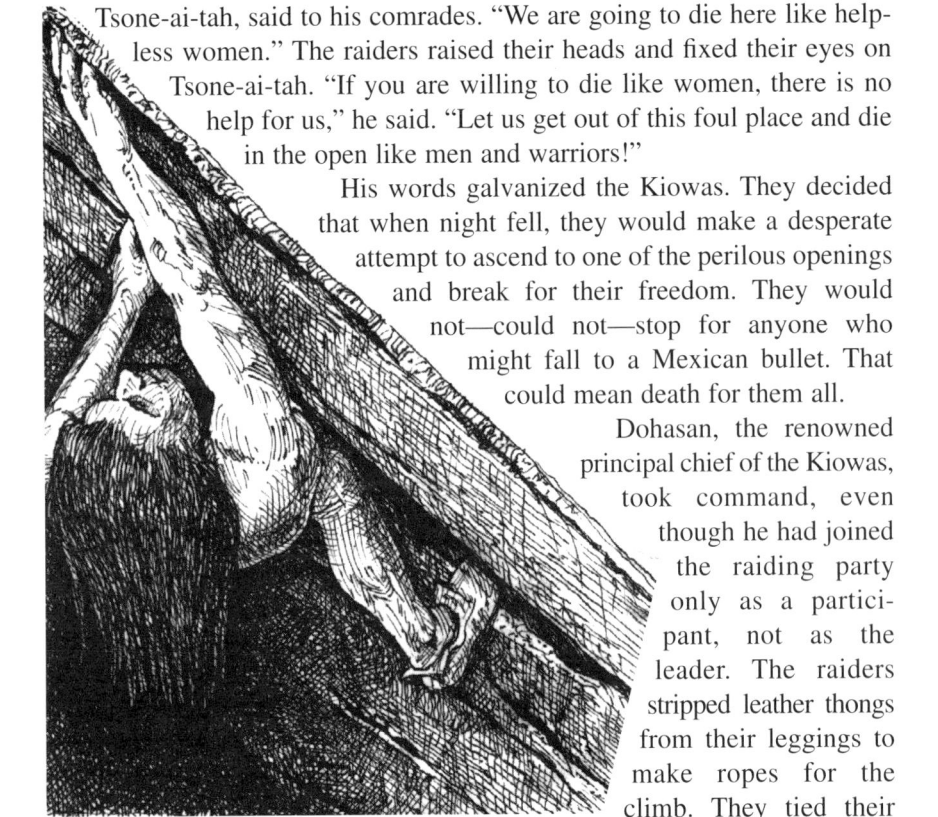

"Very well," said Dagoi, "I stay. Tell my father to come back and avenge my death." He sang his death song. He would die the next morning before the guns of the soldiers.

Dagoi, a member of the elite warrior society, the Kaitsenko, sang his death song.

Oh, sun, you remain forever, but we Kaitsenko must die.
Oh, earth, you remain forever, but we Kaitsenko must die.

The time had come.

Dohasan, silently, in the darkness, made his way up the precarious rock slope and into the night air. He extended his bow back like a lifeline to haul up the others in their ascent. One by one, he helped them to the top:

Guadalonte, who was the original leader of the raiding party;

Konate, who was about to begin the fateful experience that would grow into legend;

Hone-geah-tau-te, who would endure a searing experience of his own in the escape attempt;

Tsone-ai-tah, who inspired the raiders to attempt the escape;

Au-tone-a-kee, whose brother was the raider who died from gunshot wounds the first day of the siege.

Finally, all the Kiowas except the doomed Dagoi had climbed through the mouth of the opening. They could see the Mexicans' campfires burning on the surrounding hills.

Suddenly, a slight noise drew a shot into the darkness from one of the soldiers, and Konate felt the shocking pain of a bullet smash through his body.

At that moment Konate could scarcely have envisioned what fate now had in store for him.

Another shot, and Hone-geah-tau-te fell on the rocky hillside, no longer able to move, though, astonishingly, he would survive a scalping and brutal torture by the militia and would eventually recover and return home.

The Kiowas made no more noise. The wounded men held their silence in spite of their agony. The firing ceased.

With Dohasan in the lead, the warriors, with Konate struggling desperately to keep up, made their way as silently as specters through the darkness over a saddle in the hills and down to the desert floor. There, they stole Mexican horses, turned east through a pass in the Hueco Mountains and raced through the night into the following day and freedom. Their remarkable courage and endurance had given them a chance.

Almost certainly, as the Hueco Mountains and the Mexican militia receded, the Kiowas fled across a traditional Indian trail. If they could elude the militia, the trail would carry them eastward over West Texas desert basinland, with its scattered stands of bunchgrass, creosote, yucca, and lechuguilla; across the salt basins that parallel the western slopes of the Guadalupe Mountains and that mark the location of ancient lake beds; up through the rocky pass between the Guadalupe and Delaware Mountain ranges; down to the Pecos River, where they would cross a ford near the Texas–New Mexico border; through windblown sand dunes sparsely covered with shinnery oak, mesquites, and little bluestem grass; and then northward, toward home, along the eastern side of the Llano Estacado escarpment, where the rivers, bordered by juniper and buffalo currant, spill from the high plains and flow southeastward across rolling plains toward the Gulf of Mexico.

A day out of Hueco Tanks, the Kiowas reached a hill where they had left spare horses and supplies, guarded by two young boys, en route to the aborted raid on El Paso. The foresight proved to be a lifesaver for the raiders, for they arrived suffering from the ordeal of the siege. They had ridden the stolen Mexican horses to exhaustion. They came burdened with Konate, whose untreated and now festering wounds seemed to drain him of his life. Uncertain whether trouble lay behind them, they rested only for the night.

The following morning, the Kiowas, replenished, pushed toward home on fresh horses, putting the threat of the Mexican military behind them for good. Their troubles, however, were not over. As they reached a spring near the summit of a promontory that they called Sun Mountain, for the glisten of its stone crest in the sunlight, it became evident that the suffering Konate could go no farther. He had lapsed into unconsciousness. His infected wounds and fevered body made it certain, the Kiowas believed, that death would take him within hours.

They placed Konate within reach of the water of the spring. They surrounded him with stones to ward off scavengers anxious to eat his flesh and savage his bones. They built an arbor to shade him through his final hours. They rode away in sadness, never expecting to see Konate alive again. In accordance with Kiowa custom, they planned to send a party back from home to recover his bones and return them for burial.

Hours passed. Shadows lengthened. The desert heat softened. Konate emerged from the darkness of unconsciousness.

He discovered that he lay in absolute aloneness, left behind in the desert. He knew that his companions had headed for home, expecting that he would die. He believed now that he would die, a bitter fate after he had survived the siege, the shooting, the long hard ride from Hueco Tanks. He could feel the larvae of blowflies feeding in the decaying flesh of his wounds. He knew that his family would mourn, his women would cry. He knew that the members of his band, in accordance with Kiowa tradition, would kill his horses and burn his belongings. They would never speak his name again. He awaited his end.

As darkness enveloped the land like a black cloak drawn from the eastern to the western horizon, Konate, at the edge of consciousness, could hear the desert's chorus of nocturnal sounds. Perhaps the light click of a mule deer's hooves striking stone as it stole cautiously to the spring for water. The yelps of coyotes as they hunted down their evening meal. The startled cry of a doomed desert cottontail as it fell victim to the talons of a great horned owl.

Then, Konate heard the howl of a gray wolf, distant and unearthly.

Silence. The temperature of the dry desert air began to fall as night closed its grip.

Konate heard the voice of the wolf again, this time closer.

He realized the animal could smell the foul odor of his wounds. He lay helpless, unable to rise, chilled by the awareness that the animal could attack and dismember him, still alive, for his flesh.

On the edge of consciousness, Konate heard the wolf snuffling at the stones that surrounded him. Konate braced for the savage attack that he felt sure would come. He heard the wolf climb over the rock wall, but instead of attacking, the animal lay down gently beside him. It warmed him in the chill desert night. It licked his wounds, trying to clean them.

At daylight, the wolf disappeared, but when night fell again, it returned, perfectly gentle, protective.

Four days and nights passed. Growing weaker, drifting in and out of consciousness, Konate heard from some distant place the faint trilling of eagle-bone flutes and the song of his warrior society. The sounds drew nearer and nearer as though carried on a gently swirling wind from the spirit world to a point directly above him. A vision of Tai-me, the god of the Sun Dance, appeared before him. "I . . . shall not let you die." Konate heard the words quite clearly. "You shall see your home and friends again."

In the darkness of night by the spring, Tai-me gave to Konate special mystical powers, or "medicine." Tai-me gave him instructions for making a new war shield. He directed Konate to create a sacred staff that would serve as proof and symbol of new power. As he departed, Tai-me told Konate, "Help is near." Tai-me sent a heavy rain to cool Konate and wash his wounds.

The wolf returned in the night and resumed its vigil.

Konate heard horses approaching in the darkness. The wolf disappeared. Konate would never see the animal again.

He heard Comanche voices. Unable to speak, he groaned to make himself heard.

The Comanches, a raiding party of six warriors headed south and west on the Indian trail, were astonished to discover Konate still alive. Several days earlier, they had met Dohasan and the Kiowa raiders on the trail headed north toward home. The Kiowas asked the Comanches to cover Konate's body to protect it from wolves until a party could be sent back to recover the bones. No one anticipated that it would be a wolf that would save Konate's life.

The Comanches gave Konate water and buffalo meat broth. They cut away his filthy and bloodstained clothes. They bathed him and dressed his wounds with buffalo tallow, then dressed him in clean clothes. They cared him for several days, until he recovered enough strength to travel. They gave up their journey to raid and placed the Kiowa warrior on a shaded travois behind a gentle horse and turned north to take Konate home . . . home!

Within a few days, Konate had healed enough to sit on a horse, and he rode with the Comanches. Once again, he saw the southwest wind ripple the vast sea of buffalo and grama grasses, the great herds of buffalo and the bands of antelope. He heard the gobble of wild turkeys, the call of the bobwhite quail, the scream of golden eagles, the yelps of hunting coyotes, the howls of gray wolves.

One day, as the party drew nearer the Kiowa homeland, Konate crested a gentle rise and discovered, driven into the prairie soil, the icon of Tai-me. He realized that it represented the vision of Tai-me that had appeared before him by the spring at Sun Mountain.

The Comanches told Konate that the icon had been captured by one of their warriors from the Crows in a raid years earlier. Its Comanche owner had been killed in battle. His family discarded the icon on the trail. Konate was free to take it.

When, at last, Konate rode with his rescuers and his Tai-me icon into his home camp, his band and family erupted with joy to see him alive. They held a feast and dance for the six Comanche warriors. They gave them many horses. The Kiowas and Comanches strengthened their alliance.

Konate never forgot his experience nor Tai-me's commands. With his new medicine, his spirituality evolved and deepened. He rose to a venerated place in the Sun Dances, his story becoming a parable for the annual celebration of renewal. Perhaps more than anyone else Konate cherished the tribal gathering, the friendships rekindled, the great tepee circle, the festiveness, the feasts, young women and warriors riding together, the medicine lodge rise, the sacrificial buffalo-hide offering, the Kiowa warriors dancing to the sounds of drums and eagle-bone flutes.

He played an integral role in the medicine lodge ceremonies. The Sun Dance chief took his place and unveiled and displayed the tribal Tai-me in the medicine lodge. Konate unveiled and displayed his special Tai-me icon next to the tribe's icon. As Tai-me had commanded, he made a new war shield. He made a sacred staff, an adorned forked stick of stripped and seasoned chinaberry wood, as the symbol of his medicine. It, too, became an icon of Kiowa spirituality.

In 1849, the year before Konate died of the great cholera epidemic that swept across the plains that year, he gave the staff to a nephew, Co-yante. At the 1857 Sun Dance, held on the Arkansas River in Oklahoma eighteen years after the siege at Hueco Tanks, Co-yante sacrificed Konate's staff, driving the forked end into the earth inside the medicine lodge.

A year later, Co-yante returned to the site. He discovered that the staff had been reversed, with the forked end pointing toward the sky. Konate's seasoned chinaberry staff, cut and stripped of its bark years before Co-yante's sacrifice, had sprouted leaves. Ten years later, in 1868, it had flourished, growing into a full tree, a memorial to that terrible ordeal in western Texas so long ago, a haunting reminder of Konate's mystical experience in the desert, a monument to the endurance of the human species.

Postscript
In the summer of 1997, the rangers at the Texas Parks and Wildlife Hueco Tanks State Historical Park invited my family and me to attend their annual interpretive fair.

While there, I chanced to meet Dewey Tsonetokoy, a Kiowa who I learned to my delight is the great-great-grandson of Dohasan, the principal chief who led the raiding party out of its entrapment during the siege at Hueco Tanks in 1839. Dewey introduced me to his seventeen-year-old son, Scott, and to his sister and niece. I introduced his family to my wife, Martha, and to my youngest son's wife, Terry.

Later in the day, Terry and I met Dewey and his family members at the mouth of the amphitheater where the Mexican militia had trapped the raiders. (My wife had stayed behind to listen to mariachis.) Scott carried a coil of rope. At that moment I did not understand why.

We hiked into the amphitheater, between its towering hills, past Comanche Cave on the right, where the Kiowas were encamped when the militia attacked, through deep grass, where the Kiowa horses had grazed, past the pool where Dagoi had been shot, to the caves, deep in the amphitheater, where the raiders had endured the siege.

Dewey stopped us before we entered the caves. "Kiowa warriors died here," he said. "We can feel their spirits. We mlust have a ceremony."

Near the site where the Mexican militia dropped rattlesnakes to the amphitheater floor, Dewey conducted a brief ritual called the "smoking ceremony" in remembrance of Dagoi and Au-tone-a-kee's brother, then we crawled through the mouth and into the chambers of the cave.

We explored the labyrinth of stone, then we sought out and followed the long passageway that led to the ascending shaft and the opening where the Mexicans frustrated the Kiowa escape attempt. We could see a fleck of blue daylight sky piercing the darkness at the top of the shaft. Over the years, the rush of rainwater had apparently reopened the escape route. There appeared to be just enough room to writhe through to the surface. I suddenly understood why Scott carried the rope.

Terry and I, feeling that we might be intruding on something important to Dewey and his family, left the caves and returned to the park headquarters.

I learned later from Dewey that his son, Scott, the great-great-great-grandson of Dohasan, had successfully ascended the shaft, clinging to handholds twenty-five feet above the cave floor, negotiating a ledge no more than four inches wide, working his way upward inches at a time, and finally emerging through the opening at the top of the hill above the cave.

"I very nearly cried," said Dewey. "I was seeing something they had seen a hundred fifty years ago. It was a revelation for me."

Scott's success earned him a Kiowa name, Hay-Gal-Oop Gal-Oye-Tope, or He Went Through and Came Out.

True Believer

"You're writing a book about stuff no one can explain in Texas, and you're not going to tell about the Marfa Lights?" asked Mr. Jefferies. The aging but still vigorous gentleman smiled at me elfishly, like a kind and venerable professor indulging a misguided student. With eyes as alert and bright as those of a gray fox, he looked at me intently through wire-rim glasses. I couldn't understand why Mr. Jefferies would take an interest in what I would include in the book. I didn't even know how he knew about the book, which I had named *Texas Unexplained*.

I had just met Mr. Jefferies. He walked through the white double front doors into the early-morning coolness of the Rexall drugstore, on the west side of Marfa's Lincoln Street, just after I did. He sat down at the counter, on the stool next to mine. He wore a tired and rumpled dark blue suit with a vest and watch chain, a white shirt with a navy blue tie, a black felt dress hat with a small snap brim, and black high-top dress shoes with black laces. Brown spots of age marked the backs of his hands. He reminded me of businessmen and lawyers I used to see around courthouse squares in Panhandle farm and ranch towns when I was a youngster back in the 1940's.

The only two customers in the drugstore, we both ordered coffee. I wondered how Mr. Jefferies knew that I had decided not to include anything about the Marfa Lights in *Texas Unexplained*. That felt strange.

"Why aren't you going to write about them?" he asked with a gentle insistence, as if he were about to take a student on a voyage of intellectual discovery.

"I'm getting frustrated," I said. "I'm working on a tight deadline. I've spent five days here, and I haven't seen any lights yet. I need to work on other stories. I thought this would be a good story, but I'm beginning to wonder if the Marfa Lights really exist."

"You drove the nine or ten miles east out Highway 90, toward Alpine, to the viewing site pullout about sunset, and you looked beyond the old Marfa airfield across Mitchell Flats toward the Chinati Mountains and you didn't see the lights?"

"Four nights in a row I went there. My wife and I stood behind a big double fence, and we looked out across the Chihuahuan Desert for hours. We climbed on top of a boulder and used a spotting scope and binoculars. We saw headlights and taillights of automobiles on Highway 67, the one that runs from Marfa down to Presidio. That was all."

"Did anyone else see the Marfa Lights?"

Somehow, I could see that he knew the answer before I even responded.

"Other people claimed they saw the lights," I said. "We didn't see anything but car lights. Nothing else. Just car lights. I heard a man say that he once saw the lights drifting past the pullout, just on the other side of the fence, and he said that a light followed a friend of his home one night, right up to the garage. Scary thing."

I noticed that Gladys, our waitress and the only other person in the drugstore, looked at me as if I were a cockroach crawling among the white dishes on the countertop. "Are you okay?" she asked me. She seemed to think something strange was going on. She paid no attention to Mr. Jefferies. A late-middle-aged woman, Gladys wore a starched and pressed pale blue dress with a white apron and a hard plastic name tag.

"I'm all right," I said, puzzled by her question.

"You know what Ernest Hemingway once said?" I asked Mr. Jefferies. "He said that writing should make 'a whole new thing truer than anything true and alive.' That's what I want to do. I can't do that if I haven't even seen the lights."

Mr. Jefferies said, "Mr. Hemingway used to say a lot of things like that about writing. He talked about making things truer than true in that interview with George Plimpton for the *Paris Review* in 1958. I guess it's a good trick if you can do it."

I wondered how this aging man in an isolated town with no more than two or three thousand souls in West Texas' Chihuahuan Desert happened to know about Hemingway's interview with Plimpton.

"I used to read a lot," said Mr. Jefferies, as though he had read my mind. "Still do. You know what Mark Twain once said? He said, 'I don't believe these details are right but I don't care a rap. They will do just as well as the facts.' In a way, he said the same thing as Hemingway, only better. Getting the essence of a story right is more important than getting every single fact exactly right."

"What does that have to do with the Marfa Lights?"

Gladys looked at me out of the corner of her eye, as though she were utterly mystified, maybe even getting a little apprehensive. "Mister, are you sure you're all right?"

I ignored her question, but I could see her watching me carefully.

"Maybe I could have some more coffee?" I asked her.

"Me, too," said Mr. Jefferies.

Gladys filled our cups.

"Mysteries are important things," said Mr. Jefferies, returning to my question about the essence of a story and the Marfa Lights, "too important to be left in the hands of those people who just worry about the mere accuracy of details. A good mystery can light up the whole landscape of the human spirit."

"What do you mean?"

"Mysteries, especially enduring mysteries like the Marfa Lights, evoke stories that define the human character. We try to explain mysteries with stories about things that concern and describe us as individuals. The longing for the reunion of separated lovers, families, and communities. The consequences of betrayed faith. The sorrow caused by treachery and conflict. Fear of the unknown. Dreams of treasure always just out of reach. The good or evil of things we can't understand. Mysteries teach us about ourselves. That's why they are important."

"I still don't understand."

"Take love, for instance. That lies at the core of the human purpose. A lot of people say the Marfa Lights are lovers who are searching for each other in the darkness of desert nights after they became separated by some tragedy."

Mr. Jefferies pushed his black felt hat back on his head.

"One story tells of a beautiful Indian girl who rendezvoused with her warrior lover in the evenings in the Chinati Mountains. One night before he arrived, she saw a burst of light on a distant slope. Her warrior failed to appear. Terrified, she rushed to the slope and searched desperately for her love, finding nothing but scorched earth where the light had appeared.

"Days passed. Months passed. She saw more flashes of light in the evenings in the Chinatis. She returned to the flanks of the mountains time and again to continue what everyone knew was an utterly futile search for her lover. She rejected all the other warriors who tried over the months to court her.

"One evening as she searched the Chinatis, a burst of light as bright as the noontime sun blinded her. Even sightless, she refused to give up her hopeless quest. Day after day, she kept searching, feeling her way along the trails. Then one night she plunged over a rocky cliff to her death. The lights we see today are the ghosts of the girl and her warrior continuing their eternal search for each other."

"That's good theater," I said. "It sounds almost like operatic tragedy. It embodies a romantic notion of love and hope in the human community."

"You need more coffee?" Gladys asked me, studying me closely.

"No. No, thanks," I said.

"There are also tales of betrayal of faith," said Mr. Jefferies. "Once, years ago, a man and his wife traveled into the Chinatis, and she fell ill, too sick to travel any farther. Her husband left her and rushed into town, supposedly for a doctor. He never returned. He had abandoned her. Left her to die alone in the mountains. Her spirit still waves the lights to signal her location, hoping that her husband may yet return for her."

"What a miserable jerk that guy was," I said.

"He violated her trust, but she never gives up hope," Mr. Jefferies pointed out.

"Conflict and treachery. There are lots of stories about conflict and treachery, stories about man's inhumanity to man," said Mr. Jefferies. "That seems to be a perpetual state of affairs for the human species, and it flows through several of the tales people tell about the Marfa Lights.

"In one instance, a party of Spaniards, probably slavers, invited an Apache chief named Alsate and his band to a parley. At the meeting site, the Spaniards ambushed the Apaches. They massacred every one but Alsate. He escaped to the Chinatis. Now, what we see are the fires that Alsate, alone in the mountains, lights each night to call his followers home.

"A lot of other stories tell of man's eternal struggle to bring closure to events and circumstances that will never yield to closure.

"The lights serve as beacons for the ghosts of Indian chiefs who search the mountains for their lost followers, of sons who search for their lost fathers, of a sheriff who searches for the murderers of his wife, of a mother who searches for her lost children, of Indian sinners who wait out their penance.

"Good mysteries summon up fears of the unknown and the unknowable. An old trapper reported that he saw the lights many times when he worked his line in the Chinatis. They always illuminated the ghostly figure of a woman who beckoned to him to follow her deep into the mountains.

"The trapper declined the invitation."

"I had no idea there were so many stories," I said.

"Hundreds, maybe," said Mr. Jefferies, "and more all the time. Elton Miles tells dozens of them in his *Tales of the Big Bend,* including most of what I have just told you.

"Some Marfa Lights tales are so bizarre you can scarcely imagine their origins. Some people believe that the lights are a vengeful Adolf Hitler searching for German World War II prisoners who chose to forsake the Fatherland for America. More recently, somebody has even claimed that the spirit of James Dean has returned to Marfa and caused the lights to change color."

"James Dean?" I asked.

"James Dean, the same one who starred in the movie *Giant* when it was shot out here back in 1955. He later got killed in a car wreck," said Mr. Jefferies.

"Sure you don't want more coffee, Mister?" Gladys asked me. I had forgotten about her.

"No. No more coffee. Thanks."

"Naturally, there are lost-treasure stories," Mr. Jefferies said, "tales that the lights are Indian spirits guarding Spanish gold, that they are reflections from a cache of rare gems buried with a beautiful Indian woman."

"Has anyone ever found any treasure?" I asked.

"Lots of people. The lights themselves are a treasure," he said.

"Mr. Jefferies, I read somewhere that the lights are 'good.' I read somewhere else that they're 'evil.' What do you think? Good or evil?"

"Both."

"Both?"

"Sure. Just like people. Miles tells how the lights—benevolent— once guided a lost and freezing cowboy to shelter and safety. On the other hand, the lights—evil—have blinded drivers at night and nearly caused horrendous accidents on Highway 90."

"Do you believe any of these stories?" I asked, smiling, perhaps a little smug, believing that I knew his answer ahead of time.

"All of them," said Mr. Jefferies.

"All of them?" How could anyone believe all of them? I asked myself. That was not the answer I expected. "Why are there so many different stories?"

"Everyone sees the lights in different ways. They mean different things to different people. They tell the stories that stir their own souls.

"Some people see the lights as glowing spheres of orange, pink, yellow, green, blue, or white. The spheres behave almost as if they were tethered by some cosmological force, form out of nothingness and intensify in brilliance. Sometimes they pulsate. Sometimes they divide, like living cells, into two or four spheres. They hold their brilliance for a few moments, then begin to fade. Sometimes they reappear and repeat the performance.

"Other people see points of light, white, intense as a strobe. Sometimes a single light. Sometimes multiple lights. They often flash like micrometeorites, or 'shooting stars,' entering the earth's atmosphere in the night, except they flash across the desert floor or along the mountain flanks. Diagonally sometimes, horizontally sometimes. They describe circles, zigzags. They bob up and down, like a bouncing ball. They pulsate rapidly, disappear, reappear. A few people even believe the lights are young witches, just learning to fly. I like that one.

"People stand side by side and see different things at the same moment. Some see the lights just once and never see them again. Others see them sometimes but not other times.

"Of course, some people never see them at all." Mr. Jefferies looked at me and smiled indulgently. I knew one of those he was talking about.

"Scientists must have investigated the lights. What do they think?"

"People have known about the lights for more than a hundred years, and scientists have studied them at least since World War II, when the U.S. Army ran the air base out by Highway 90. Elton Miles says that the military reportedly sent airplanes, helicopters, and Jeeps out to investigate the lights. Supposedly airplanes crashed, helicopters exploded, Jeeps burned, and soldiers disappeared. The military just cleared out after the war.

"Academics from all over the place have come to Marfa to study the lights. They can't offer any explanation, mostly just speculation and theory."

"What kind of speculation and theory?" I asked.

"I've read more than thirty scientific explanations for the lights.

"The UFO boys believe they are navigational lights or some kind of

Morse code for space aliens. Other people believe they are just moonlight reflecting off mica or silver deposits, or the flash of meteorites or comets, or bones, coal deposits, or bat guano glowing in the dark, or luminescence from some kind of chemicals left by the army after World War II.

"My favorite explanation is phosphorescent rabbits."

"Phosphorescent rabbits?" I tried to imagine phosphorescent rabbits darting across the mountainside in the darkness, uncomfortably visible to hunting coyotes.

"Rabbits that glow in the dark. I've always liked luminescent bunnies," Mr. Jefferies said.

"The more scientific type of folks have suggested a whole other array of explanations.

"Swamp gas, for example. We know that methane generated by decaying plant material can glow, especially in swamps."

"Swamp gas?" I said. "But that's a desert out there. Not a swamp."

"St. Elmo's fire," Mr. Jefferies said. "That's another explanation scientists have suggested. You may have seen it shrouding something like an airplane's wings or a flagpole. It's an electrical halo that glows, usually when air masses with different temperatures collide and create static electrical charges in the air. Scary stuff when you're on an airplane during an electrical storm."

"The Marfa Lights occur during cloudy and clear nights both. Couldn't be St. Elmo's fire."

"There's earthquake lights."

"What are earthquake lights?" I had begun to get confused by all the explanations.

"As you might expect from the name, earthquake lights occur when there is an earthquake. Many people have seen them, particularly in those parts of the world where they have a lot of earthquakes. Some scientists think the lights may occur when static electrical charges are built up by rocks grinding against each other under the surface of the earth."

"But Marfa doesn't have an earthquake nearly every night."

"Let's try mirages. They can occur in the sky when a blanket of cold air overlays a blanket of warm air. The boundary between the blankets acts as a reflector of objects, sometimes from a long distance away. People have seen mirages in the sky of whole cities, oases, caravans, even armies."

"That doesn't seem like a logical explanation for the Marfa Lights. No one sees cities or camels. Just lights."

"I'm running out of potential explanations," said Mr. Jefferies, smiling slightly, as if he were amused by the whole exercise, "but some scientists think the lights may be 'ball lightning.'"

"What?" I wasn't sure I had heard Mr. Jefferies correctly.

"Ball lightning," he repeated. "Few people have even seen ball lightning. It behaves like a drifting bubble of light. It usually occurs around sources of high voltage. Storm lightning. Large battery installations. It's eerie stuff. Ball lightning has been reported to pass intact through solid walls and windows.

"Some think ball lightning is a sphere of glowing plasma trapped by electromagnetic forces. Others think it's glowing gases released from some living object struck by lightning. One scientist thinks it may occur when thunderstorms produce high-energy radio waves that interact and convert air into a glowing plasma. It may be, of course, no more than an optical illusion, that kind of image you retain in your eye after a sudden brilliant flash—an 'afterimage.' Fact is, no one can say that the Marfa Lights are ball lightning. No one really even knows what ball lightning is. It's like explaining a mystery with another mystery."

"Which of all those theories do you believe is the most likely explanation for the Marfa Lights?" I asked.

"None of them."

"You believe all those stories ordinary people tell about love, betrayal, treachery, fear, and all the rest, and you don't believe any of the theories scientists have developed after serious investigations?"

"None of them. Except maybe the phosphorescent rabbits. I've always been partial to luminescent rabbits."

"Do you think the mystery of the Marfa Lights will ever be solved?"

"I hope not. We need mystery."

"Somehow, I get a feeling that you know the real explanation, Mr. Jefferies."

"I've known it for many years."

"For God's sake, tell me!" I said, my voice rising.

"Mister, can I call a doctor for you?" interrupted Gladys, alarmed.

I turned to Gladys, annoyed by the anxious tone of her voice. "Why would you call a doctor for me?"

"You're getting all excited," she said. "I can call a doctor!"

I turned back to where Mr. Jefferies had sat. To my astonishment, his stool was now vacant, his coffee cup gone, as though no one had ever been there. What happened to him? He was there just a moment ago.

"Where did he go so quickly?" I asked Gladys.

"Where did who go?" asked Gladys. "You've been talking to yourself for the last half hour. I'm getting worried about you."

"What happened to Mr. Jefferies?"

"Mister Jefferies? Are you certain you're okay? You've been talking to empty space."

"Yes, I'm fine. No doctor."

I looked again at Mr. Jefferies' stool. Empty. No coffee cup. I suddenly felt rattled and confused. What could have happened to this kind and wise old gentleman who had told me about the Marfa Lights and luminescent bunnies? He had disappeared as suddenly as a shooting star in an evening sky.

"I'll leave now," I said.

"No need to pay for the coffee," said Gladys. She sounded as if she were anxious for me to get out of there. "It's on the house."

"That's very kind. By the way, who is Mr. Jefferies?" I asked.

"Mr. Jefferies?" said Gladys. She paused for a long moment.

"Who is Mr. Jefferies?" I prompted.

Gladys spoke very softly. "Mr. Jefferies taught people about rocks and stuff like that at Sul Ross University over in Alpine back in the 1940's. He was there for years. Everyone in this area knew him in those days. He disappeared one night, up in the Chinati Mountains. He often went up there to look for the lights. He became obsessed. People warned him not to go up into the mountains at night by himself at his age. But he went up there that night. No one ever heard from him again. He just vanished. How did you know about him?"

"I think I met him once," I said.

I walked out of the drugstore. A block and half to the north, on the town square, I could see Marfa's dominating, elegant old three-story French-style courthouse with its domed top crowned with a brilliant white statue. Unexpected architecture here in West Texas.

I felt the desert sun warming the back of my neck. I walked over to the historic Spanish Baroque El Paisano Hotel to meet my wife, who had run an errand.

"I just had coffee over at the Rexall Drug," I said to her.

"The Rexall Drug?" she asked.

"Sure."

"But the Rexall Drug is closed. Apparently has been for years."

"It can't be. I just had coffee there. I talked with a Mr. Jefferies about the Marfa Lights. He used to teach at Sul Ross. A woman named Gladys waited on us."

We drove slowly up Lincoln Street toward the courthouse, past the Rexall Drug with its black-tile facade. Through the large plate-glass windows on either side of the white double-front doors, I could see into the interior of the drugstore. I could see a stack of discarded fluorescent lightbulbs lying on an inside windowsill. Beyond, I could see a dusty, cavernous emptiness.

My wife looked at me out of the corner of her eye, as though she were utterly mystified, maybe even getting a little apprehensive. "Are you okay?" she asked. "I'm getting worried about you. Should we check with a doctor?"

"I'm fine," I said. I knew, though, that we had to stay over a day and go out to the viewing area again that night and look beyond the old Marfa airfield across Mitchell Flats toward the Chinati Mountains just one more time.

The Stone Heads of Malakoff

Just before noon on Saturday, November 2, 1929, Cuban-born Indelicio Morgado, his brother Teo Morgado, and several other workmen labored with picks and shovels at the bottom of a gravel pit. The pit was part of a stream-deposited terrace overlooking Cedar Creek, a tributary of Texas' Trinity River. The creek ran through Judge W. R. Bishop's farm, some fifty-five miles southeast of the heart of Dallas and five miles west of the hamlet of Malakoff, Texas. The workmen loaded the small cobbles and sand into the bucket of a hoist, which raised the load into the waiting dump trucks of the Texas Clay Products Company.

Morgado, his brother, and the other workers probably thought little of the economic collapse that had begun convulsing the nation little more than a week earlier. They probably felt thankful just to have a paying job, even one that wore heavy calluses into the palms of their hands.

On previous days, they had picked and shoveled their way through the stratum of gravel to a depth of sixteen to eighteen feet, where they reached a clay surface that just overlay the bedrock at the bottom of the deposit. They dug into the clay to improve their access to the surrounding walls of gravel.

They uncovered a boulder embedded in the soil. Strange. About the size and shape of a small watermelon, it was far larger than the river cobbles in the overlying gravel deposit. It had no apparent natural place in the clay. Indelicio Morgado freed the boulder from its earthen bed. He turned it over and found himself staring into a crudely sculpted face of stone.

The clock struck Saturday noon, the end of the workweek, and exhaustion outweighed curiosity. The head could wait where it lay in the bottom of the gravel pit for another day and a half, until the beginning of a new workweek. It had already waited for a long time.

Come Monday morning, Morgado and his men returned to the pit and their find. They loaded the stone head into the hoist bucket, lifted it to the top of the pit, and dropped it into a truck bed. The impact broke a piece off the back side, an unsculpted part of the head.

Teo Morgado rescued the head, placing it inside the truck cab, on the seat beside him. He drove to a Texas Clay Products Company construction site and dumped his load of gravel. He removed the mysterious head and set it on end, the position its sculptor might have intended.

When Texas Clay Products president T. A. Bartlett and mining engineer V. C. Doctorman saw the stone face, they, like the Morgado brothers, realized that it could only have been fashioned by the hands of an ancient craftsman, someone who had left it resting on the clay soil before the Trinity River system buried it with sand and cobbles.

Doctorman notified Dr. Elias Howard Sellards, director of the Texas Memorial Museum in Austin, of the find: "In a gravel pit about four and a half miles west of Malakoff where some workmen were excavating was found a roughly carved stone, which upon further investigation proved to be shaped very much like the human skull. Diamond-shaped openings have been carved to represent the eyes, and an attempt has been made to properly represent the ears, nose, and mouth. There is some evidence, also, that the figure was once placed upon the top of a prominence of some kind. This I assume because of a hole, or cavity, back of and underneath the chin. The fossil will probably weigh sixty-five or seventy pounds and is covered with iron oxide, which weathers very easily."

On November 26, 1929, Sellards arrived at the site to inspect the gravel pit for himself.

Indelicio Morgado showed him, Sellards said, the "depression in which the stone had rested." Sellards excavated the clay soil from several square yards around the depression, finding no "additional relics of man." Clearly, this ancient sculpture would not give up its secrets easily.

Exposed to air, the head, a sandstone concretion that in fact weighed nearly a hundred pounds, began to crumble. Sellards preserved it with an application of gum arabic, which penetrated the stone pores and cemented the grains of sand. He said, "The prominent features of the face—eyes, nose, mouth, chin, and ears—are plainly carved on the stone." He noted the cavity under the chin, possibly used "to allow a support to be inserted to hold the head upright."

There the matter rested, a mystery.

In September, 1935, a thousand feet west of the pit where the stone head was found by the Morgado brothers, a workman named Joe Gunnels opened another pit, in the same stream-deposited terrace, using a scraper drawn by a team of horses or mules. He cut completely through the terrace to the underlying clay and bedrock surface so that he could determine the deposit's depth. The blade of his scraper uncovered a boulder embedded in the soil. Strange. About the size and shape of a small watermelon, it measured far larger than the river cobbles in the overlying gravel deposit. It had no apparent natural place in the clay.

Joe Gunnels reined his team to a halt. He climbed down from the scraper to inspect the boulder. He found himself staring into a crudely sculpted face of stone. The blade of his scraper had struck the top of the head, which had been sitting upright, leaving a scar as wide as a man's hand.

Sellards, again called to the scene, used gum arabic to preserve head number two, another brittle sandstone concretion. He reported, "The second image is somewhat smaller than the first. Its weight is sixty-three and one-fourth pounds." The facial features were less distinct than those of head number one, but, said Sellards, because of a three-inch-deep notch in the back of the head, "the finished object, when viewed from the side, closely resembles a skull." Sellards believed that the notch served as a receptacle for a support.

There the matter of the two stone heads of Malakoff remained, still a mystery.

How long had they rested in the bed of clay? No one could say.

Who had sculpted these images in stone? No one could say.

What did they mean to the sculptors' people? No one could say.

In April 1938, nearly eight and a half years after Indelicio Morgado discovered the first head, scholars returned to the river terrace to see whether they might solve the riddle of the heads.

Financed by the University of Texas and the Depression-era Works Progress Administration—the WPA—they expanded Sellards' initial excavation in the clay bottom of Morgado's pit. After twenty months of work, they finally found a third brittle, melon-size sandstone concretion, this one only vaguely sculpted, and larger by a third to a half than the first two. They found absolutely no other artifacts. Not a single one.

In addition to the excavation, however, they analyzed and defined the geologic context of the river terrace itself, which the flowing waters had deposited on top of the abandoned sculptures. This proved more rewarding.

They learned that the terrace was the oldest of three that the river system had laid down in the immediate area since the heads were carved. They discovered that the terrace itself contained the fossils of the great mammals of the last Ice Age, or the Pleistocene Era, which drew to a close 11,500 years ago. The stone heads had to be older than the overlying terrace with its fossils.

The geologic analysis pointed to great antiquity for the sculptures, to a time when vast fields of ice blanketed much of Canada and the northern United States; when the Gulf coast lay miles south of today's shoreline; when annual rain and snowfall declined and deserts expanded across the Southwest; when large mammals, many now extinct, occupied North American prairies and woodlands.

Sellards wrote: "The age [of the sculptures] in years is that represented by the lowering of the flood plain of the river sixty or seventy feet through three successive stages."

He could scarcely conclude anything more on the basis of the meager information he had.

Often, the further back in time we look, the dimmer the view of the past and the more mystifying the clues.

From evidence embedded in the earth and documents shelved in library archives, we have, for instance, a rich record of the relatively recent history of the Caddos, the federation of Indian tribes who greeted the first European explorers to north central and eastern Texas and the people whose friendly greeting "Tejas!" gave the state its name. In the western part of their range, they occupied villages in a tallgrass prairie interspersed with wooded river drainages, and in the eastern part, they lived in hamlets in the piney woods. They built beehive-shaped wooden houses, manufactured excellent pottery, tattooed their bodies, and intentionally deformed their infants' skulls. Consummate agriculturists, they raised corn, beans, squash, and sunflower seed. They believed in an omnipotent deity and built earthen mounds topped by wooden temples, the scenes of elaborate ceremonies.

If we look further back in time, to the archaeological period just preceding the time of the Caddos, to the thousand years between 200 B.C. and 800 A.D., the record grows more faint. We suspect that the Indians who occupied the upper Trinity River drainage, then a savanna not unlike that found by the earliest European visitors, introduced settled village life, pottery, the bow and arrow, and the first cemeteries to the region. They made an array of tools of stone, shell, and bone. Only rudimentary agriculturists, they relied heavily on hunting, especially for white-tailed deer and rabbits, and on gathered foods, especially hickory nuts, for subsistence. We know little of their political system or their religious beliefs, although archaeologists infer that they provided some origins for Caddoan political structures and religion.

If we look still further back in time, from 6,000 B.C. to 200 B.C., a period before settled villages or pottery or the bow and arrow, the record grows even dimmer. We see the outlines of a people—nomadic seasonal hunters and gatherers—adapting to a world that was emerging slowly and fitfully from the end of the age of ice. They occupied a land, in the upper Trinity River Basin, in which the Ice Age forest was giving way to the more modern savanna. They usually lived in small bands, moving from hunting camp to hunting camp. They preyed on bison and antelope, stalking them until a hunter could drive home his stone-point-tipped spear. They harvested wild plants, newly abundant because of the changing climate, processing them with grinding stones, cooking them in stone-lined fire hearths and baking pits. They made their projectile points and tool kits from locally available rock. We know little to nothing of their religious beliefs and ceremony. We can only guess, on the basis of ephemeral clues we can see in other cultures of comparable development, that the upper Trinity hunters and gatherers were a profoundly spiritual people.

If we look further yet back into the prehistory of the upper Trinity, to a time when ice still covered much of Canada and the northern United States, to the moment when an early sculptor carved facial features into the sandstone concretions at Malakoff, the record becomes faint and fragmentary. We see widely scattered and shadowy small bands of predominantly big-game hunters who occupied a land covered with open forests and populated with huge mammals.

As suggested by the fossils embedded in the gravel stratum that overlay the stone heads, these early people shared the landscape with mammoths, mastodons, bison, llama-like camels, horses, the giant ground sloth, and other mammals. These animals would have towered above those of Caddoan times.

The mammoths and mastodons stood ten to twelve feet at the shoulder and weighed six to eight tons, as much as four automobiles. The ancient bison had a horn span more than three times that of modern bison. The giant ground sloth stood as large as a modern ox.

Far-ranging and nomadic, the hunting bands of the period surrounded and killed with such efficiency that they appear to have extinguished entire species of the great animals from the land.

They depended on their prey so completely that—and this is utter speculation—they developed a religious system intended to assure success in the hunt. Other comparable cultures equated spirituality with the animals and plants essential to their survival.

The big-game hunters of north central Texas valued their hunting weapons so highly that—and this is utter fact—they either quarried or traded for the highest-quality flint and chert from lithic sources as far away as the Texas Panhandle and Hill Country and the New Mexico desert. They knapped stone spear points from the materials with the same care that a diamond cutter fashions beautiful carbon crystals. The projectile points they left behind reflect some of the highest lithic craftsmanship anywhere in the prehistoric world. They are works of art in the genre.

Unfortunately, the fossil record, widely scattered Ice Age campsites, occasional Ice Age game-kill sites, and isolated exquisite projectile points constitute only a few pieces of the jigsaw-puzzle picture of a past people. Archaeologists and anthropologists cannot, for example, yet identify with certainty the ancestors of the Ice Age people of the upper Trinity River drainage nor of the Americas in general. They cannot yet pinpoint with certainty the origins of the ancestors or their entry routes into the Americas. These are age-old questions in American archaeology and anthropology.

When the stone heads of Malakoff surfaced, they raised hopes that new pieces of the puzzle might emerge. Instead, they raised more questions.

When in the Ice Age did the sculptor(s) carve the stone heads of Malakoff?

Why did he, she, or they carve figures too large for a nomadic people to carry with them in their never-ceasing journeys across the land?

Why did the people leave them in this particular area on the upper Trinity River, apparently isolated, with no other artifacts?

What, if anything, do the sculptures, rudely shaped like a human skull, have to tell us about the beliefs of the early residents of America?

Do other similar Ice Age sculptures still await discovery?

The mystery of the stone heads seemed confounded by irony.

The discovery itself seemed almost preordained. In two instances, a thousand feet and six years apart, workmen who presumably knew little if anything about Ice Age archaeology or geology just happened to dig in locations where the heads lay buried. They just happened to notice something "different" in the pits where they worked. In a time when Americans felt far more concerned about earning a living than about discovering the past, workmen retrieved the heads. Managers notified experts. They changed the work schedules of their crews to permit investigation. The landowner, Judge Bishop, encouraged the studies.

Yet there the trail ends. The heads have never yielded any information beyond the fact that they were carved by the hands of Ice Age people in the upper Trinity River drainage.

Two of the stone heads of Malakoff, enigmatic as ever, now rest in storage in the Texas Memorial Museum in Austin. The third head remains in private hands.

Archaeologists will likely never return for further investigations in the gravel river terrace that yielded up the heads. For today it lies submerged beneath the waters of the Cedar Creek Reservoir.

INTERVIEW WITH CHEETWAH

"I've never told this story to anyone before now," said Cheetwah. He had materialized out of nowhere. "I'm going to tell you because you are the first journalist who ever took me seriously enough to come up here and look for me. I trust that you will report truthfully. It's important that we finally get this history right. I want to set the record straight. That's never been done before this."

He looked straight into my face, wanting to be sure I understood. "Remember, I have a lot of power," he said.

I had hiked to Indian Springs, located up a V-shaped canyon on the east side of El Paso's Franklin Mountains, where the state park is today, to find Cheetwah. I read in a yellowing old newspaper that his spirit hung out there and that you could see the profile of his face on the peak just above the springs.

Cheetwah, taller than most Indians, lowered himself to a seat on a boulder and leaned back against the trunk of a small soapberry tree, making himself comfortable. He wore a breechcloth of deerskin and sandals of yucca fibers. A large disk-shaped gold gorget was suspended from his neck by a leather thong. Since he took the only available boulder, I had to sit on the ground, looking up at him. I took out my notebook so I could record his story.

"How did you find out about me?" he asked.

"I read about you in J. Frank Dobie's story about the Lost Padre Mine here in the Franklin Mountains. He said that you were chief of an ancient tribe of Indians and that you summoned up all the warriors in the spirit world to exterminate the Spaniards when they lived here. After that, you took your people into the mountains and just vanished, and now you protect the Lost Padre Mine from the treasure hunters. You're famous. Anyone who looks for the Lost Padre Mine knows about Cheetwah. Some people say you won't ever let anyone find it."

"Or any of the other treasures in the Franklin Mountains, up until now," said Cheetwah.

"There are other treasures?"

"I'm going to tell you about them in my own good time. Don't get impatient."

"Sorry."

"Dobie got it pretty close—he was a good storyteller—but I was around a long time before the Spaniards came. When I was a little boy, all we used to do was hunt mountain sheep and mule deer here in the mountains and catch catfish down there in the Rio Grande. It was a pretty good life.

"One day some fellows came up here from somewhere down south. southern Mexico or Central America, they said. They talked about some great big buildings down there that they called temples. They wanted to swap us some green feathers and these little copper bells and stuff for some turquoise. We thought that was a pretty good deal. Turquoise was cheap here, so we traded, and after a while it got to be a regular thing."

"Wait a minute," I said. "How long have you been around here?"

"I don't know. Maybe fifteen hundred years. Time goes pretty fast."

"That's hard to believe," I said.

"We learned a lot from those fellows," Cheetwah continued. "We started planting some corn and beans and squash—I never did learn to like squash—that they brought up here. We kept on hunting and fishing. We had more to eat. Life got even better. After a while, though, we got tired of living in holes in the ground with just branches and mud for a roof—'pit houses' they call them nowadays—so we built us some places like those Indians up north and northwest of here have built the last few hundred years."

"You mean the Pueblos?" I asked.

"Of course," he said.

"What about the treasures?"

"Don't get impatient. I'm going to tell you."

The sun had dropped behind the mountains now, and I wanted to get the story and learn about the treasures and get out of Indian Springs before darkness fell. It's hard walking in the dark. Besides, I didn't want to miss *Wheel of Fortune*.

"Like I say," Cheetwah continued, "we had it pretty good. We even found us a big gold mine here in the Franklin Mountains, and we dug out some gold and made big gorgets, like mine here, that we could hang around our necks. We looked swell."

"Where is the mine?"

Cheetwah ignored my question. "Then one day, in about the year 1535, as I recall, these four strange-looking people with beards turned up. They came out of the east. They sure weren't Indians, but there was a bunch of Indians following them. The leader was a man named de Vaca, or something like that, and there was a dark-skinned fellow. I forget his name."

"Cabeza de Vaca and Estevanico?"

"That sounds about right. I got kind of worried even back then because they asked a lot of questions about our cities and gold and silver."

"Did you tell them where your gold mine is located?" I asked, hoping he would tell me, too.

Cheetwah ignored my question. I had a feeling he was just putting me off. "I think that fellow Cabeza de Vaca started something. Just five or six years went by and a man called Coronado—I'll never forget that name—brought a whole army of bearded people along with some Indians through Arizona and New Mexico, up north of here, and he went across through Texas and Oklahoma and clear up into Kansas, and he asked a lot of questions about our cities and gold and silver. He told us he was going to do us a favor and save our souls. By then we had found out that these bearded men were called Spaniards."

"Did anyone tell Coronado where the Lost Padre Mine is?"

Cheetwah ignored my question. "Nothing much happened for a while. Oh, a few small parties of Spaniards came around about 1580 or 1590, somewhere along in there, but most of them cleared out before too long. One time they left some men who wore long blue dresses with hoods at one of the pueblos up north. They said they were going to save some souls. They didn't last long, though. They wore out their welcome. The men in the pueblo sent them on their way to heaven. Everybody won. The pueblo got rid of the padres. The padres had a better life.

"Then in 1598—in late spring, hot, I'll never forget it—Juan de Oñate shows up at the Rio Grande River, about where San Elizario is today. He had at least five hundred Spaniards and probably eighty or so little wooden carts with big wooden wheels, and the men were driving at least seven thousand cattle, sheep, goats, horses, and pigs. I don't know what all. You never saw such a cloud of dust. They stretched out for a good two miles. I knew then we were in serious trouble, because they sure asked a lot of questions about our towns and gold and silver. We wanted to be friendly, so we got all painted up and wore our best gold and helped them get across the Rio Grande there where it turns through the pass between the Franklin and Juarez Mountains and heads southeast."

"I'll bet you told Oñate where the Lost Padre Mine is," I said, smiling knowingly.

Cheetwah ignored my comment. "Oñate went on up the river, toward Santa Fe, but it wasn't too many years before the Spaniards started a town right across the river from us, not far from where the old ford is located. Pretty soon, one of our people did tell the Spaniards about our gold mine, where it is and everything. He said he wanted to have his soul saved. So the padres saved his soul, and they took our mine and our gold. They seemed very pleased with themselves."

Cheetwah fell silent.

I glanced at my watch. I had already missed *Wheel*. "That's not the end of the story?"

"I'm waiting for you to ask about the treasures," he said.

"The Lost Padre Mine and all the others?"

"Of course," he said, looking at me like I was a slow learner or something. "I got mad when the padres took our mine and our gold, so like Dobie said, I put out a call for all the warriors in the spirit world, and we got together with the Pueblos up north and in 1680, we attacked the Spaniards and drove every last one of them out of New Mexico. Killed a bunch of them, too. Unfortunately, the survivors settled here around El Paso."

"Did they give back any of your gold?"

Cheetwah looked at me as if I were not only a slow learner but an idiot as well. "With all the Indian troubles, the padres got worried about the treasure the Spaniards had accumulated, so they decided to hide it up in the Franklin Mountains."

"And you know where?" I asked.

Cheetwah ignored the question. "It was a big treasure. The padres said they hid 4,336 ingots of gold, 5,000 bars of silver, nine mule loads of jewels they had stolen from the Aztecs, and some important papers they had smuggled out of Spain. It's the richest Spanish treasure in all of America. I have never told anyone this before, but I, Cheetwah, know for a fact that there were originally 4,500 ingots of gold, 5,500 bars of silver and ten mule loads of jewels. I'm the only one who knows that. I always wondered what happened to the difference."

"You don't think the padres could have taken it?" I asked in disbelief.

Cheetwah looked at me in disbelief, but I could see that he was ready to share something special with me. "Whatever happened to it," he said, "they hid the rest of the treasure, along with some gold chalices and plates and other church stuff at . . . "

"Your mine! It's at the southern end of the Franklins," I interrupted, completing the sentence for him, excited that he had finally told me. "The padres hid it and that's why they call it the Lost Padre Mine. At one time, you could see the mouth of it from the north window at the top of the bell tower at the Nuestra Señora de Guadalupe Mission church on the square in downtown Juárez. You had to look exactly at sunrise on a certain day of the year. You had to line up certain landmarks. If you knew just when and where to look, you could see the opening of the mine. I knew it! That's what Dobie said."

"That all started out as a joke," said Cheetwah. "It just got out of hand. The mine's not there. Besides, you can't see the Franklins from the mission church now anyway. The big, newer cathedral next door is in the way."

"But Dobie said that a priest from Ysleta, down the Rio Grande from El Paso, made his parishioners carry dirt, red soil, up from the river to fill in the shaft of the mine. They covered it with a big stone slab with a cross engraved on it."

"That was a different shaft. The priest did that to mislead people. The treasure is really hidden at . . . "

"Right here at Indian Springs!" I almost shouted. Now I knew. "I read that in an old edition of the *El Paso Herald Post*. Sometimes, at night, a bluish-green glow marks the location. Henry Gardiner—he used to be a caretaker out here—saw it out here in the middle of March, 1939. He said it moved eastward, grew smaller, darted into the mountain, and disappeared. Some Boy Scouts saw it that same night. A lot of people have seen it over the years. Some people are afraid to stay out here at night because of the glow."

"No," said Cheetwah. He seemed weary. "I'm beginning to think you're not at all interested in getting this story right and setting the record straight. You just want me to tell you where the treasures are, and then you can go home and eat supper and come back and get rich."

I decided that I would be more suave and subtle when I asked about the Lost Padre Mine.

"That glowing light is not the treasure," said Cheetwah. "That's me. Usually I don't materialize and let anybody see me, but my stomach glows bluish green or sometimes a reddish color when I get indigestion or frustrated. It shows at night. I can't help it. That's what people are seeing. I wish they weren't afraid. I get lonesome out here sometimes."

"If it's not at the south end of the mountains and not here at Indian Springs, it's got to be at the Canyon with the Red Doors," I said, feeling a little frustrated myself now. "That's the canyon with red sandstone at the entrance."

"Where?" asked Cheetwah, plainly puzzled.

"I'm surprised that someone hasn't found it," I said. "An awful lot of people have hiked and ridden the trails up here for an awful long time. You would think someone would have stumbled across the Lost Padre Mine."

"A lot of people have looked, and sometimes we have had to take certain precautions. We have even had to spook a few people," said Cheetwah. "Back in 1882, a Captain Jim White and W.E. Kneeland and his wife hired some prospectors to look for the mine. They spent a lot of money and never got close.

"In 1888, a couple of fellows named Robinson and Big Mick dug twenty feet of dirt out of a hole, but they didn't get close either. They dug the river dirt out of the Ysleta priest's shaft. Lot of good that did them.

"In 1890, an L. C. Chriss found a great big shaft, with a couple of tunnels forking off. He found some old Spanish stuff around there, too. It wasn't where the Lost Padre is, but we collapsed the shaft just to be on the safe side. Too bad about that fellow."

"You mean Chriss?"

"No, one of his workers. Got buried in the cave-in. He wasn't supposed to be in there."

"In the 1920's, two guys named Don Thompson and Jack Ronan flew around in an airplane over the Franklins, looking for the mine, and they thought they could see it down in a canyon. Later, they climbed up the canyon and found a big rockslide. They told everybody the mine was under the slide. We dressed one of our guys up like an old Mexican man, and they found him digging at the top of the slide. He told them he found a big slab with a cross, and then he disappeared. Thompson and Ronan dug out an awful lot of dirt looking for the mine."

"I read that they found an old Spanish chisel," I said, a little incredulously.

"We planted it there," Cheetwah said. "We were just kidding around."

"I heard that some Indians downriver from El Paso knew where the Lost Padre Mine is."

"You don't think Indians were going to tell where it is, do you? They still believed in the old ways, and they knew I would strike them dead if they told. They just said that they were good Catholics so they could get the padres off their backs."

"There sure are a lot of stories," I said. "I've read about all kinds of maps and documents and church records and treasure hunts for the mine."

"We planted a lot of the old maps and stuff," said Cheetwah, "just to confuse people."

"Well, Cheetwah, where exactly is the Lost Padre Mine? I've read that it's not even in the Franklin Mountains at all. It's located in the Hueco Mountains, way out east of El Paso, or in the Organ Mountains, up in New Mexico."

"I've tried twice to tell you. It's located up above . . . "

"I know! I know! It's in McKelligon Canyon, up above the amphitheater where they have the big musical show *Viva El Paso!* every summer. That would be the perfect place."

"It's not there." Cheetwah looked a little cross and frustrated. I could see that the conversation had cooled. He seemed tired. I thought I could see a faint bluish-green glow in the vicinity of his stomach. He must have been getting indigestion. But he seemed determined to go on.

"We do enjoy seeing *Viva El Paso!* every year," he said, brightening slightly. "We get to go free because no one knows we're around. We get good seats, too."

"Why have you kept the Lost Padre Mine all for yourselves all this time, Cheetwah?"

"Taxes."

"Taxes?"

"So we can pay our taxes. They have gone up every year since Oñate came through here in 1598. You can't imagine how much trouble he started. They claim they're going to cut taxes starting next year, though, and they're going to give us more deductions. Things should finally start to loosen up. I can finally tell someone about the treasures and get on with my spirit life."

"What about the other treasures? You said there were more. You said that you wanted to set the record straight."

I was getting a little anxious to hear the end of the story. Darkness was beginning to fall. It was going to be too late even for any of the reruns of *Wheel*. I was glad that Cheetwah had begun to speak faster, like he too wanted to get finished.

"Some people say Pancho Villa's people buried treasures up in the Franklin Mountains, but I never have found any of those. There were treasure caves, though, where some outlaws who ran with a really bad man named Slim used to hole up. His bunch used to rob wagons, stagecoaches and trains all the time. People thought those caves are up on the west side of Mount Franklin, but I can tell you that's not where they are. Anyway, we got the treasure out of them and hid it again before the U.S. Deputy Marshall, Bob Ross, found the caves in 1887. All we left was some plaster and charcoal and some other stuff that didn't have much value. Charlie Kluepfer, who used to run the Congress Saloon down in El Paso, found an old ladle at the caves. Said the outlaws used it to melt down the jewelry they stole.

"After Ross discovered those caves in 1887, Slim found himself another cave in the Franklins, and he left a lot of treasure there. We never did bother to move it, but we nearly wished we had a couple of times."

"What do you mean?" I asked.

"Back in 1900, a fellow herding sheep found the cave. He made a torch and went inside, and he found the treasure, in a big wooden box. It was full of coins and jewelry and stuff. Then he saw the mummified bodies."

"Mummified bodies?" I asked. It was really getting dark now. I decided all at once that I was getting really hungry.

"Three of them. They were swinging from the ceiling. The sheepherder took off and never came back. We didn't have to do a thing about him.

"A few years later, about 1905, Slim himself came back. He had retired from robbing people, and he brought a retired Army sergeant with him. Wanted to show the sergeant something really horrible, he said. He showed the sergeant the treasure. He claimed it was the booty from his gang's last twelve robberies. He told the sergeant that he had buried the bones of soldiers, Mexicans, Indians, and other robbers under the floor of the cave."

I got a feeling now that Cheetwah was trying to scare me, sitting there in the gathering darkness.

He said, "I stood there in the cave with them, listening to them, in case I had to do something to save the treasure. They didn't know I was there, of course. Finally, Slim showed the sergeant the three swinging mummies. 'You won't ever tell nobody about this place, will you?' Slim had a lot of really yellow teeth. Some of them were missing, and he liked to grin a lot. He grinned at the sergeant. It was downright scary. The sergeant said, 'No, I ain't never going to tell nobody about this place.'"

It had turned so dark now that I could just barely see Cheetwah. I could hardly see the light reflecting off the gold gorget hanging from his neck. He was more like a shadow. His voice seemed to be fading with the last light.

"About 1931 . . . " he said softly. I had to lean forward to hear him. ". . . a man named John L. Chester found Slim's last cave, and he went down to El Paso to get a truck so he could come back and haul out the treasure. Unfortunately, we had to arrange for Mr. Chester to have a sudden heart attack. Too bad he was a nice man. Since then, no one has come close to any of the treasures, but a lot of people are still looking. Now, that's all the treasures I know about in the Franklin Mountains."

I could barely hear Cheetwah anymore, and I thought he must be getting tired. I put away my notebook. I didn't want to overstay my welcome. I wanted to get back to El Paso and get something to eat. "People keep looking," I said. "I had a friend who told me the other day that he has just found out where the Lost Padre Mine is. He got hold of an old map and some directions. He believes that he can find it. He's got a pair of Spanish stirrups that came from somewhere close to the mine, he thinks."

I stood up. "By the way, you never did tell me the real location for the Lost Padre, and I know you want to set the record straight . . . " I looked closely at the cottonwood tree where Cheetwah had been sitting. I could just make out his fading image. I saw a momentary slight reflection from his gorget. I thought I heard him say something about "another journalist, another time." Then he was gone. He disappeared like a wisp of smoke in a West Texas wind.

I hiked down from Indian Springs, stumbling over rocks in the trail in the darkness, trying to avoid all the things that stick and bite and sting out in the desert. About halfway down, I looked back toward Indian Springs and I could see a bluish-green light up there in the night.

Postscript
If you are not afraid of the vengeful spirit of Cheetwah, you can hike, bike, and ride horseback through Franklin Mountains State Park's challenging trails. Surrounded by El Paso, at thirty-seven square miles it is the largest urban wilderness park in the nation and one of the largest in the world. Astonishingly, given the proximity of the city, you may see mule deer, gray and kit foxes, coyotes, desert cottontail rabbits, blacktail jackrabbits, and perhaps even a cougar. You will see a variety of birds, maybe even golden eagles. You will discover that the flanks of the mountains are covered with classic Chihuahuan Desert plant life, including lechuguilla, sotol, ocotillo, various yucca and cacti, and, uniquely in Texas, the Southwest barrel cactus. The fall of the year, especially around October, is the ideal time to explore the Franklins.

The Mystery of the Lady in Blue

MISSION DE ISLETA

Young Nun Teleported to New Spain?
(Filed May 21, 1626)
TxUnexpl News Service

    AGREDA, SPAIN—A reliable source, speaking on condition of anonymity, reports from this small village 130 miles northeast of Madrid that the spirit of Sister María Jesús of Agreda, a twenty-four-year-old nun of Saint Francis's Poor Clares, has "flown" by teleportation hundreds of times over the past six years to minister to Indians in New Spain, especially to the Tejas and Jumano tribes in that vast and little-known region in the eastern part of the northern frontier.
    Sister María, according to the source, has long grieved for these Indians, whose souls suffer the eternal torment of hell because they know nothing of Christianity.
    During her spiritual visits, she claims that she instructs the Indians—in their own languages—in the fundamentals of the Faith. She heals the sick. She has persuaded many to accept the teachings of the Church. She urges the Indians to call on the Franciscan missionaries of New Mexico to carry the word of God eastward.
    Sister María brings such devotion to her calling that she says she is prepared to offer her life in return for saving a single Indian soul.
    Since she became a nun, at the age of seventeen, she has prayed almost constantly for the Indians. She has had visions and trances in which she sees the Indians and their lands. She has seen God, who speaks to her of the need to minister to the Indians.
    Our source reports that Sister María experienced her very first trance one day following a holy communion. As she knelt, she grew pale. She

The Mystery of the Lady in Blue

swayed, lost consciousness. A beggar who witnessed the event said that a brilliant blue light enveloped her body, which levitated several feet above the floor. Soon, her trances followed nearly every communion. Levitation followed every trance.

Finally, in 1620, the year of her eighteenth birthday, Sister María entered a trance as she prayed at the foot of the Cross, and she found herself, for the first time, in a strange new land, in the presence of bronze-skinned men and women. She had experienced "bi-location." Her body had remained in one place while her spirit and consciousness traveled by teleportation to another.

She had seen the earth divide into day and night, felt the temperature of the air around her change. She realized that the people were the Indians she had seen in her earlier visions and trances. She reported that they used animal teeth and jawbones to fashion weapons.

God directed her to take His message to these people.

Now, six years later, the source says, Sister María, always wearing the heavy blue sackcloth cloak of her Franciscan order, continues her flights to minister to the Indians at least four times a month and, on some occasions, two or three times a day.

Often, she says, she has felt unworthy to carry out God's order. She has had a sense of bewilderment. She has wondered whether she has dreamed her experiences. As a test, she took rosaries from her cell for her spirit to give to the Indians during one of her flights. When her spirit returned to her body, she searched for the rosaries, which she never found. This confirmed her belief in her mission.

Although she has had many successes, she says that at least once she failed to gain converts. She won martyrdom on the banks of the Colorado River, west of New Mexico, when warriors shot down her spirit with arrows as she spoke to them. She collapsed, then rose to her feet and disappeared into the sky.

Sister María, however, refuses to let even her most arduous experiences divert her from her mission. She says that she will continue her ministrations for as long as God wills.

Now that they are reported, Sister María's fantastic claims will lift the hopes of the Church and especially the Franciscans, who, symbolic of Spain's profound religious fervor, passionately seek to convert the native peoples of New Spain.

Her claims, however, will also raise questions about her credibility, especially in seventeenth-century Spain, where religion casts such a powerful spell over the people, from the nation's royalty to the most poverty-stricken, and mysticism has such taken deep root and is now glorified.

Sister María must prove her right to follow in the traditions of those giants of mysticism such as Saint Teresa of Avila, Saint John of the Cross and El Greco. They have woven an enduring Spanish heritage.

Decades before Sister María was even born, Saint Teresa experienced an ecstatic trance and heard a voice command her to speak no more to mortals, only to angels. She founded the cloistered order of the barefoot Carmelites and committed herself to prayer and humility. She became canonized only a few decades after her death.

Saint John of the Cross, one of Saint Teresa's protégés, helped her found the new barefoot order. Angry traditional Carmelites kidnapped and imprisoned him. In a dark cell, his mysticism bloomed like the red spring poppies of the Spanish countryside. Upon his release, Saint John, with Saint Teresa, raised mysticism to the pinnacle of the nation's religious consciousness.

El Greco, the artistic soul of Toledo in the late sixteenth century, gave visual expression to the nation's religious and mystic beliefs. He painted elongated figures of such piety that they seemed to rise from the dark surfaces of his canvases like souls ascending into heaven.

Such mystics resonate with the soul of seventeenth-century Spain, and now the Spanish people and especially the Inquisition will challenge anyone professing similar mystic credentials.

Sister María takes great risks. If she proves her claims, she could become venerated as a saint. If she fails, she could be burned at the stake as a witch.

We must wait to see what effects, if any, her ministrations in the northeastern frontier of New Spain may have on the fortunes of the land.

Whatever else she may be, Sister María is a brave woman.

• • •

Young Nun Appointed Convent Abbess
(Filed November 30, 1627)
TxUnexpl News Service

MADRID, SPAIN—Reports reaching this capital city from the small village of Agreda, 130 miles northeast of Madrid, confirm that Sister María Jesús of Agreda, a twenty-five-year-old nun at the Poor Clares' Concepción Purísima de Agreda Convent, has recently been elevated to abbess, an appointment that required special papal dispensation because of the nun's youth.

Sister, now "Mother," María has gained fame in recent years because of her claim, so far unsubstantiated, that her spirit flies frequently by teleportation to minister to the Indians in New Spain, particularly in the mysterious northeastern frontier region.

Her venture into mysticism, which holds such a prominent place in Spain's religious landscape in this seventeenth century, appears to have begun the day she was born María Coronel, on April 2, 1602. The new infant, called a "special blessing" by her mother, Catherine Coronel, caused far less pain by her emergence into this world than her siblings caused by their births.

María grew up in privileged surroundings. Noble Spanish blood flows through her veins. Her family, including her two brothers and a sister, has enjoyed an aristocratic lifestyle. Her father, Francis Coronel, has owned the largest castle in their entire province of Soria.

By the time María reached two years old, her mother suspected that her child might be a prodigy. The little girl had surprising ability to reason.

By the time she reached four, María began hearing voices from God. She played and spoke with friends invisible to her mother and father. At six, her compassion for the poor had surfaced. Her obsession with the spiritual world flowered.

As time passed, María mystified her parents, who began to think of their own child as "strange," in fact, as a burden. They refused to believe her explanations for the voices and her invisible friends. They expressed their disapproval and disappointment with her avoidance of the patrician life at the family castle. They imposed a strict discipline on the child.

María soon came to feel unloved and rejected by her mother and father. She withdrew to her own ethereal corners of life. She declined physically and grew sickly.

The child nevertheless possessed a steely inner strength, deciding at the age of eight that she would become a nun. At twelve, she won her parents' approval and prepared to enter the Sisters of Teresa's Convent of Saint

Ann, located at the nearby city of Tarazona.

At that moment God intervened, redirecting María's life forever.

Her mother, Catherine, who had thought her daughter's mysticism strange, experienced a vision of her own. It came during prayer. A voice directed that the family should give its possessions to the poor and convert its ancestral castle into a convent for the Franciscan order's Poor Clares. The voice said that she and her two daughters should enter the convent and that her husband, Francis, should enter a Franciscan monastery as her two sons had already done.

María, thrilled, deferred the start of her life as a nun so that she could enter the new convent at her own home instead of the Sisters of Teresa's Convent.

On January 13, 1620, with the convent at Coronel castle completed, María, her mother, and her sister took their vows. Her father entered a Franciscan monastery as a lay brother.

María, by this time a beautiful young woman, became Sister María Jesús of Agreda.

The cloistered life of the Poor Clares, striving for continual union with God, has resonated with Mother María's soul. In accordance with the practices of their order, Mother María and her sister nuns arise at midnight, the first canonical hour of the day, to pray for the poor, the suffering, the dying (and, in Mother María's case, for the Indians). They work diligently throughout the day—writing, painting, cooking, sweeping, mending, gardening—to demonstrate their obedience, safeguard their chastity, and procure God's glory.

Ironically, accordingly to a highly reliable source familiar with the convent, Mother María, when an novitiate, suffered terribly at the hands of her abbess and the other nuns, who mocked her piety and misunderstood her mysticism.

Under the pressure, reports our source, Mother María became haunted by apparitions—the ghosts of lost souls, the misty figures of living people, the shadows of savage animals. As she struggled to control her demons, her health deteriorated. She retreated to pray in private. In spite of her torment, she forgave her sister nuns, prayed for them, loved them.

Disturbed, her abbess called for an ecclesiastical examination for Mother María. Father Anthorn de Villacre questioned her at length, and to the astonishment of her sister nuns, he declared that Mother María had achieved the true sanctity for which all of them yearned. The moment marked a turning point in Mother María's life.

The abbess and the other nuns, horrified by the injustices they had committed, replaced mockery and misunderstanding with esteem and veneration, so much so that Mother María grew embarrassed by their attentions.

Free of harassment, she soared into ecstasy. She began her spiritual quests, in the blue cloak of her order, with the Indians of New Spain. She took an increasingly important role in the affairs of her convent. It was her success which led the Pope himself to approve her appointment, at her extraordinarily young age, to abbess when the post came open earlier this year.

Clearly, this young nun has overcome difficult trials of the spirit. She has attained a level of sanctity which is extraordinary at any age. It is my opinion, however, that Mother María's real trials have just begun.

With her ascendancy to abbess, there is even greater urgency to verify her fantastic claim that her spirit travels by teleportation, or what the Church calls "bi-location," to minister to the Indians of New Spain, and there is no better place to confirm her story than in that vast land of the northeastern frontier, a region populated by tribes who have never seen a Franciscan friar or other Catholic missionary.

So far, we have only the barest glimpses of the area and its native people.

We have Cabeza de Vaca's century-old record in which he reports on his wandering journey westward across the land from the Gulf of Mexico to New Mexico and ultimately into Mexico. He speaks of the long coastline with its marshes, huge shallow bays, and barrier islands. He reports on inland trails, broken lands, arid mountains, scrub forests, and prickly pear cactus. He tells of fowl, deer, and large black-horned beasts.

We know from the reports of Moscoso, who assumed the leadership of the survivors of the De Soto expedition, that the northeasternmost corner of the wilderness is gently rolling land covered by a pine forest.

We know from the chronicles of Francisco Vázquez de Coronado's expedition in the 1540's and Juan de Oñate's expedition at the turn of the century that a high, featureless, flat, plain cut deeply by widely separated rivers lies due east of New Mexico. This region supports many grazing herds and predatory animals.

We know, too, from those early explorations that a large array of tribes—hunters, gatherers, raiders, fishermen, farmers—speaking various languages populate the land. They knew nothing of Christianity from the time of Cabeza de Vaca through Juan de Oñate, before the presumed appearance of the spirit of Mother María.

The region offers an exceptional chance to investigate and authenticate Mother María's stories. If her claims can be proved true, the Church will be presented with unique new opportunities to convert these lost souls to the nation's faith, a surpassingly important mission of Christianity.

As a novitiate, Mother María stood trial before the nuns of her Convent.

As an abbess, this young nun must now stand trial before the Church itself, the Inquisition, the Spanish empire.

The issue lies at the core of the Spanish soul.

• • •

**Franciscan Effort to Verify Mother María's Claims
(Filed April 30, 1630)
TxUnexpl News Service**

MEXICO CITY, MEXICO—Reports circulating through this capital city recently indicate that Franciscan officials have uncovered significant new evidence about a young Spanish nun's claims that her spirit flies frequently by teleportation to teach Christianity to the Indians of the northern frontier.

The nun, Mother María Jesús of Agreda, twenty-eight years old, has served as abbess in the Poor Clare Concepción Purísima of Agreda Convent, located in the small village of Agreda some 130 miles northwest of Madrid, for the past three years. She says that, although physically she has never left the village, the place of her birth, her spirit has traveled through teleportation—"bi-location" as the church calls it—hundreds of times since 1620 to minister to the Indians.

Don Francisco Manzo y Zúñiga, Archbishop in Mexico City, learned of her story from a letter from a Spanish priest who knows Mother María. The archbishop decided to investigate.

He drafted a letter to the Franciscans serving in New Mexico. He told them Mother María's story, saying that she had even reported names of tribes she had visited, including one called the Titlas (possibly the "Tejas" Indians, suggested the archbishop) and another called the Jumanos. He directed the friars to report back to him about any tribes they found in the eastern wilderness who had learned of the Catholic faith from some source that could not be traced back to the missionaries themselves.

He dispatched the letter with Father Esteban Perea and thirty Franciscan friars and lay brothers, who were about to undertake the long trek northward to begin missionary service on the northern frontier.

Father Perea would relieve Father Alonso de Benavides, Superior of the Franciscan Missions of New Mexico since 1622 and a man who had won wide recognition for his courage and talent under the hardships of the frontier. The thirty friars and lay brothers, supplied by Philip IV, King of Spain, would bolster those already serving and expand the Franciscan missionary effort.

The reinforcements underscore Spain's growing realization that the northern frontier may yield little in immediate wealth for the crown but that it offers a rich opportunity for recruiting new souls into the Catholic faith.

When Father Perea and his fellow missionaries reached New Mexico, they met Father Benavides on July 22, 1629, at the new Mission San Antonio at the Isleta Pueblo, in the heart of the frontier region. They promptly reviewed the archbishop's letter.

The Franciscans realized immediately that they had chanced upon a strange coincidence. For even as the fathers opened the letter, the principal chief and some fifty representatives of a people the Spaniards called Jumanos—the exact name of one of the tribes visited by the spirit of Mother María—were encamped at the mission.

They had come to Mission San Antonio at Isleta as directed by a "Lady in Blue," they claimed, to request that missionaries be sent to minister to their people, located hundreds of miles to the east. They wished to be baptized and to live as Christians.

Father Benavides recalled that the Jumanos had come to the mission every summer since 1620—the year of Mother María's first spiritual visit to New Spain—in increasing numbers to plead for missionaries. Benavides had never had enough friars to meet their request.

This year, the Indians seemed convinced, would be the time in which missionaries would finally come to them.

Fray Juan de Salas, who had served with Father Benavides on the frontier for years and spoke several Indian dialects, recalled that the Indians had told him in previous summers of the Lady in Blue. He had dismissed the story as unbelievable. No young Spanish woman, especially a nun, would be permitted to venture into the wilderness alone. He thought the Jumanos must have heard about Christianity by word of mouth from other Indians. Could Fray Salas have been wrong?

The Franciscans went directly to meet with the Jumanos. Fray Garcia de San Francisco, one of the new friars, showed the Indians a small painting of Mother Luisa of Carrion, herself a Poor Clare nun who dressed in the blue cloak of her order. They asked the Indians, does this look like your

Lady in Blue?

No, the Jumanos responded. Our woman is younger, very beautiful, but she wears a blue cloak identical to the one in the picture. She arrives not by horse but from the sky, the Indians added. Could the Lady in Blue be anyone other than the spirit of Mother María Jesús of Agreda?

Father Perea knew that he had to investigate further. He decided to dispatch a small expedition to accompany the Jumanos on their return to their home.

He recruited Fray Juan de Salas and Fray Diego Lopez and three soldiers—all the troops the Franciscans could spare—for the journey. Within days, the five Spaniards and the Jumano delegation turned eastward out of the Isleta mission.

Here some confusion sets in. The Franciscans call a number of the tribes in the wilderness to the east by the name of Jumano, apparently using it as a somewhat generalized term. By contrast, other people call a specific tribe that lives along the Rio Grande and in the southern buffalo plains by the name of Jumano. Consequently, we do not know for certain which tribe the Spaniards accompanied. We will have to await further word.

We do know that the party, as it traveled hundreds of miles eastward, crossed over arid mountain passes and intervening desert basins, forded the Pecos River, trekked across the buffalo plains and through a rolling prairie to a site south of the river whose waters carry the reddish sediments of the land upstream.

At this point, the party was met by contingent of twelve Jumanos who had been dispatched from the tribal village and who, mysteriously, seemed to know in advance exactly where and when the encounter would occur. Somehow, without prompting, the Indians knew to venerate the crosses hanging from the priests' necks. They knew to kneel and kiss the hems of the robes worn by the priests. Were these clues that the Lady in Blue had, in fact, visited their villages and instructed them in Catholic behavior?

The twelve emissaries pleaded with the party to hasten to the village, which was suffering because water holes had dried up and game had abandoned the area. The people faced impending starvation. Many had wanted to move the village immediately to a more prosperous location, but the tribe, in spite of warnings from the shamans, decided to postpone a move briefly in anticipation of the long-awaited arrival of Franciscan priests, who—according to their Lady in Blue—would appear within a matter of days.

The Indians then dispatched the twelve, who were respected members of the village, to meet the priests and their party at the site near the river, the location where the Lady in Blue said the encounter would occur.

The arrival of the party at the village a few days later sparked joyous celebration. At last, missionaries! The friars were greeted with two wooden crosses, garlanded with flowers. The Indians said that the Lady in Blue herself had helped attach the blooms.

During the next several days, the friars conducted morning and afternoon masses; taught prayer; baptized men, women, and children; healed the sick.

Meanwhile, neighboring tribes, who had also been touched by the Lady in Blue, sent their representatives to the village to plead for visits to their villages as well. None showed greater persistence than those from a tribe called the Tejas.

The friars, however, had to return to New Mexico. They needed supplies. They felt anxious to report their experiences with the Indians and the evidence for the Lady in Blue to Fathers Perea and Benavides. They promised the Indians that the Franciscans would come back to build permanent missions.

Father Benavides has now returned to Mexico City and reported the details of this story to the archbishop. His evidence so far appears to substantiate Mother María's claims that her spirit has flown hundreds of times by teleportation to teach Christianity to the Indians in the wilderness. Father Benavides plans next to travel to Spain and seek an interview with Mother María herself at her convent in Agreda to investigate the story further.

It appears that the stage is being set for an expansion eastward of the Franciscan missionary effort. We will have to wait and see whether a nun who has lived all of her physical life in the small village of Agreda in northern Spain will prompt the nation to expand its missionary effort in a faraway land that she has visited only in spirit.

• • •

Benavides Interviews Mother María, the Lady in Blue
(Filed August 15, 1631)
TxUnexpl News Service

MADRID, SPAIN—Within the past month, reliable sources here have reported that Father Alonso de Benavides, former Superior of the Franciscan Missions of New Mexico, held extensive interviews with the well-known mystic, Mother María Jesús of Agreda, Abbess of the Poor Clares' Concepción Purísima of Agreda Convent in northern Spain, during the first two weeks of May.

He sought confirmation of stories by New Spain's northeastern frontier

Indians that the twenty-nine-year-old nun, whom they call the Lady in Blue, has paid them numerous miraculous visits for several years to teach them about Christianity.

Benavides reports that Mother María "has a beautiful face, very white, although rosy, with large black eyes." She wears the Franciscan habit with a cloak of heavy blue sackcloth.

Mother María spoke of her "grief for those who are damned . . . who, because of the lack of light and preachers, do not know God, our Lord." She said, during trances, she has "flown" to the Indians to minister to them more than five hundred times since 1620.

"She told me so many tales of this country," said Benavides, "that I did not even remember them myself, and she brought them back to my mind."

To his surprise, Benavides learned that the spirit of Mother María attended his baptism of the Piro Indians, remaining invisible throughout the service.

Her spirit, again invisible, also helped Father Cristobal Quiros, a friar who served under Benavides in New Mexico, with baptisms of Indians. She described him quite accurately, saying that "although he was old he did not show any gray hair, but that he was long-faced and ruddy." She helped manage the crowd of Indians, pushing them into their places so the friar could proceed with the baptisms without interference. The Indians laughed because they could not see who urged them forward so insistently

Mother María confirmed that her spirit had sent Jumanos to the Mission San Antonio at Isleta for years to plead for missionaries to raise the Christian banner in the lands to the east. She knew the details of a journey that Fathers Juan de Salas and Fray Diego Lopez and three soldiers made with Jumano emissaries to visit their village hundreds of miles east of New Mexico in 1629. She described the five Spaniards with accuracy. She visited in spirit many times, she said, with the Jumanos and other tribes to teach them about Christ, but she traveled most frequently farther east, to the land of the Titlas tribe (a name that may be her mispronunciation of the word "Tejas," according to some, including Don Francisco Manzo y Zúñiga, Archbishop in Mexico City). The archbishop's interpretation tends to be supported by reports from the wilderness saying that the Tejas Indians have long petitioned the Church to send missionaries to the tribe's lands to baptize and Christianize the people.

Mother María gave many other details about numerous tribes during the course of the interview with Benavides in May, all apparently confirming that she is, in fact, the famed "Lady in Blue."

And as if more verification were needed, she had told the story of her teleportations to the reverend father general, Father Bernardino de Sena, several years before Benavides ever left his post in New Mexico.

Benevides is preparing a report on his interview, and he will send it to his missionary colleagues in New Mexico.

He will also include a letter from Mother María herself. In it, she speaks to the role of God in her mission, and she says, "Perhaps He chooses the most insignificant and unworthy individual to show the strength of His mighty hand so that the living may know that all things derive from the hand of the Father of Light dwelling on high, and that we attain everything through the power and strength of the Almighty. And so I say that this is what befell me in the provinces of New Mexico, Quivira, the Jumanos, and other nations, although these were not the first kingdoms where I was taken by the will of God."

It seems clear, in the year 1631, that Mother María has prepared the way for the Franciscans to extend their missionary efforts into the eastern reaches of the northern frontier.

• • •

The Legacy of Mother María, the Lady in Blue
(Filed April 30, 1720)
TxUnexpl News Service

MISSION SAN ANTONIO DE VALERO (THE ALAMO)—Mother María Jesús of Agreda, the famous "Lady in Blue," still casts the mysterious shadow of her spiritual presence across the Franciscan missionary efforts here on the northeastern frontier even though she died more than half a century ago and she never in her lifetime physically left the Spanish village of Agreda.

In fact, through more than five hundred spiritual visits through teleportation to minister to the Indians in the wilderness from 1620 (a century ago this year) to 1631, she prepared the way and became a catalyst for the expansion of the mission system across Texas.

She taught her charges the rudiments of Catholicism. She encouraged them to contact Franciscan fathers and appeal for missionaries to travel to tribal lands to build churches and teach Christianity. She, with the Indians, convinced skeptical Franciscans of the truth of her spiritual ministry. Her work fired the Fransciscans' enthusiasm for converting the souls of the Indians of Texas.

In spite of the Indians' pleas and the friars' enthusiasm, the missionary activity here in the northeast has moved at a slow tempo. In 1629 and again in 1631, Fray Juan de Salas led missionary expeditions to the lands of the Jumanos, one of the tribes that responded most persistently to Mother María's message. In 1634, Alonso de Vaca led another expedition eastward from New Mexico into the Texas wilderness to respond to Indian pleas for missionaries. Little missionary activity took place thereafter for four decades, when friars led expeditions across the lower Rio Grande into Texas, and they began to plan for other missionary activities.

The early missionary expeditions, inspired by Mother María, did, however, break a trail for other Spanish interests in Texas. Spaniards began trading with the Indians of the buffalo plains. They looked for a possible route to connect Texas with their Florida colonies. They searched the Concho River for freshwater pearls. Shamelessly, they raided tribes for slaves to work Spanish fields and serve Spanish households.

Finally, in the 1680's, the Spanish learned that the French, under La Salle, had appeared in Texas.

The Franciscan desire to save souls and the crown's desire to secure Texas suddenly converged. Spain soon forged a strategy for settling the land: Construct missions in strategic locations where Indians could be congregated, converted, taught, and settled in Spanish-controlled communities. Build and man presidios to protect the missions and growing communities.

What better place to begin than in the far eastern part of the northern frontier, in the heart of the land of the Tejas Indians? The spirit of Mother María had spent more time ministering to the Tejas than to any of the many other tribes she visited. Prepared by Mother María for Christianity, the Tejas had petitioned frequently for missionaries.

"They are very familiar with the fact that there is only one true God, and that he is in Heaven, and that he was born of the Holy Virgin," said Alonso de Leon, who led an exploratory expedition into Texas in 1689. "They perform many Christian rites, and the Indian governor asked me for ministers to instruct them, [saying] that many years ago a woman went inland to instruct them."

In 1690, a quarter of a century after Mother María's death, three priests and 111 soldiers arrived in the tribal lands. They built a crude wooden church and living quarters, dedicating the new mission, San Francisco de los Tejas, on June 1. Almost before the friars could begin their work, disease, drought, and starvation laid a heavy and deadly hand on the mission. Tejas died by the thousands. The Spaniards abandoned the mission on October 25, 1693.

The missionary effort in Texas languished for more than two decades. Prodded by another French incursion, the Spanish have now begun constructing a great arc of missions that will reach from Mexico to Louisiana.

San Antonio de Valero, the Alamo, was constructed as a way station mission here on the San Antonio River just two years ago. A new mission, San José, has just been founded about five miles downstream.

We appear to be approaching the zenith of the missionary period in Texas, although the Franciscan fathers, the military, and the settlers must overcome a tidal wave of problems if they are to succeed.

They face isolation from any support by Mexico. They must recruit, settle, train, and Christianize Indians who have no tradition of permanent villages or the European values. They must face the ferocious threats of the Comanches, Apaches, and other tribes from the north and west. They must rely on an undisciplined and unruly military force. They visit European diseases, often with deadly effects, upon the Indians, the very people whose souls they would save. Ultimately, they cannot count even on Spain, once a great nation, but now in a spiraling decline.

It is a monumental task for those who would bring Christianity and civilization to the Indians of Texas.

Still, they feel sustained by the legacy of Mother María, who is still recalled by the Indians themselves.

In 1690, more than half a century after Mother María's last spiritual visit to the northern frontier and during a visit by the famed Jesuit missionary Father Eusebio Kino and Father Juan Matheo Manje to the Pima, Yuma, and other villages to the west of New Mexico, the Indians told them, according to Manje, "A beautiful white woman carrying a cross came to their lands. She was dressed in white, gray, and blue. . . . She spoke to them, shouted, and harangued them. . . . The tribes of the Rio Colorado shot her with arrows and twice left her for dead. But coming to life, she left by air."

Again in 1690, a Tejas chief asked Don Damian Manzanet, one of the Franciscan missionaries, for a piece of blue baize in which to bury his mother. He specified blue, the missionary said, "because in times past they had been visited frequently by a very beautiful woman, who used to come down from the heights, dressed in blue garments, and they wished to be like that woman."

To this day, Mother María lives in tribal memories.

Although she never came to the Indians in her physical person, Mother María Jesús de Agreda has become the spiritual founder of the missionary movement in the land of Texas.

• • •

The Lady in Blue, Her Enduring Mysteries
(Filed December 15, 1991)
TxUnexpl News Service

AGREDA, SPAIN—The mysteries surrounding Mother María Jesús de Agreda, whose body lies here in a crypt in the Poor Clare convent, where she died in 1665, have endured, unexplained, for well over three centuries.

A mystic who experienced many visions and trances, she rose to fame in the seventeenth century, when she claimed that her spirit visited and ministered to the Indians of New Spain's northern frontier, especially the Texas region, more than five hundred times. Both the Indians and Mother María offered substantial proof of her claims. No one has been able to refute her story.

Now we can add another mystery that no one can explain. Her body, like those of a few other mystics and Catholic saints, has never decayed, although she has been dead for three and a quarter centuries.

Scientists and doctors examined her body in 1909. They found no indication of decomposition. A Spanish physician examined her body again in 1989, and he said this year: "What surprised me about this case is that when we compared the state of the body, as it was described in the medical report from 1909, with how it appeared in 1989, we realized it had absolutely not deteriorated at all in the last eighty years."

Her body endures in a Spanish crypt in this small village in northern Spain, at the convent where she served. Her spirit lives in the great landscape of Texas mystery and legend.

The Lady in Blue remains as mysterious in death as in life.

• • •

THE STRANGE ODYSSEY OF THE GOOD SHIP *LIVELY*

WRECK OF THE *LIVELY*

The third week of November, 1821.

Stephen F. Austin had explained the mission of his newly acquired sailing ship, a small schooner named the *Lively*, quite clearly: Transport a vanguard of immigrants, including their equipment, provisions, and crop seeds, from New Orleans in the United States to his new colony in the state of Coahuila, the land of Texas, in Mexico. He anticipated that this would be the first of a number of such voyages for the little vessel.

According to plans, the *Lively* would depart from New Orleans and sail through the inland waterways out into the Gulf of Mexico. Once in open waters she would turn to starboard, to the west, and follow the northern Gulf coastline past the mouth of the Sabine River, which formed the border between Mexico and the United States in 1821; past the twenty-eight-mile-long barrier island of Galveston, which appeared on Austin's earliest maps of the region; past the mouth of the Brazos River, which rose in the fabled buffalo plains hundreds of miles to the northwest; to the mouth of the Colorado River, which was Austin's designated landing site.

With reasonably good luck and decent winds, the *Lively* should complete the voyage of roughly five hundred miles in five to ten days.

Meanwhile, Austin would lead another party of immigrants with equipment, provisions, and livestock on an overland route, westward across the Old San Antonio Road, from Nacogdoches to the territory embraced by the Brazos and Colorado Rivers. This was the land granted to him by the Mexican government for colonization. He would rendezvous with the *Lively*'s immigrants at the mouth of the Colorado River as soon as he could get there.

Everyone, ship's crew and immigrants, understood the plan and the objective.

Stephen F. Austin's great adventure, the settling of south central Texas, could now begin.

Mexico encouraged settlement because it wanted to strengthen its hold on Texas and discourage U.S. aggression. Ironically, the strategy backfired. It led not to a stronger grip but to the revolution in which the names of the Alamo, Goliad, and San Jacinto would enter the lexicon of legends of heroism and freedom. It was a result that Austin could scarcely have foreseen as he helped unleash the wave of immigration from the United States to Mexican Texas.

Stephen F. Austin, barely twenty-eight years old, certainly did not think of revolution that November. He had inherited the role of colonizer from his father, Moses Austin, who had died only six months earlier. The young Austin had to move swiftly to consolidate his position.

By August 1821 he had traveled to San Antonio and secured confirmation from Governor Antonio Martinez that, under Mexican law, the son became heir to the right of the father's colonization grant contracts with the Mexican government. By September, he had explored south central Texas and chosen the land for his colony. By October, he had advertised for colonists in the United States and created a wave of excitement, both for Austin and for potential immigrants.

There was a lot at stake. The Mexican government had promised to reward Austin with 23,000 acres of land for every 100 families he attracted to Texas. It would grant each family some 4,600 acres in return for a mere $190 in fees for legal documents and a survey.

Austin's new colony sounded like a utopia to potential immigrants. Magnolias, numerous oak species, and loblolly pine growing along the river bottoms would furnish building materials and firewood. The tall and medium grasses of the prairies would provide grazing for cattle and horses. Fertile soils held out the promise of bountiful corn, cotton, and, possibly, sugarcane crops and of fine vegetable and flower gardens. Warm weather, especially the mild winters, meant long growing seasons. Abundant bison, antelope, white-tailed deer, rabbits, squirrels, turkeys, mourning doves and bobwhite quail from the land, as well as speckled trout, flounder, redfish, black drum, catfish, and other species from the Gulf coastal waters would grace settlers' tables.

Most potential colonists felt little concern about the Karankawas, seasonal hunters and gatherers who had occupied the land for centuries; or about Mexican laws, which required that new citizens pledge allegiance to the Mexican flag and faith to the Roman Catholic Church; or about wilderness life, with its realities of hardship, isolation, and risk. Opportunity blinded them to caution.

To Austin and his earliest immigrants, the schooner *Lively*, though small, must have seemed like the ideal instrument to spearhead his great enterprise. A journey by ship would require only a few days; a journey by land, three to six weeks. A journey by ship involved comparatively little physical stress; a journey by land meant demanding cross-country treks or horseback or wagon rides over a wilderness trail. A journey by ship skirted Indian threats; a journey by land crossed numerous tribal ranges, each with the threat of attack.

Schooners like the *Lively* had long since proven their worth. In 1821 they functioned like ocean going passenger/freight trains. They served the open seas and coastal areas of the Gulf. Schooners had two or more masts. The height of the rear mast always equaled or exceeded the height of the forward mast(s), and this was the identifying marker for this class of sailing vessel.

The eighty-four ton, two-masted *Lively* measured fifty-nine feet in length and eighteen feet in width. She had a draft of only nine feet, making her ideally suited for service in the shallow waters of the coastline and bays of the Gulf coast of Texas. She had a cabin for the crew, and a second deck, especially constructed just above the freight holds, for the immigrants.

Austin purchased the *Lively*, in partnership with a New Orleans resident named J. H. Hawkins, for six hundred dollars. One of the immigrant passengers, an experienced frontiersman named Edward Lovelace, loaned Austin and Hawkins most of the money for the purchase.

By mid-November, Austin and Hawkins had virtually completed arrangements for the voyage of the *Lively*, and Austin left New Orleans for Nacogdoches and the overland journey west.

Although the *Lively*'s captain had not yet appeared, her crew members loaded their vessel with its cargo—farm implements and tools, crop seeds, iron and pot metal—the currency of a new colony. They provisioned her with mess pork, bacon, salt, flour, Irish potatoes, sea bread, rice, and lard. They welcomed anxious immigrants who came to inspect the vessel. The

"Little *Lively*," the immigrants called her affectionately.

The crew also stowed trunks that belonged to Austin and that contained "some things" for Governor Martinez and "his lady." Hawkins asked later, "Did the little presents to our friends meet the welcome hoped for?" Apparently, Austin and Hawkins understood the political realities of the Texas frontier.

Near the end of the third week in November, the crew had the *Lively* ready to receive her passengers, with their high expectations, their soaring optimism.

It was then that the captain, a man named Cannon, recent skipper of a two-masted vessel, or brig, out of Rhode Island, arrived to take command, just at breakfast time.

Hired by Captain Rinker, one of the ship's creditors, Cannon, about fifty years old, stood some five and a half feet tall. His bloated, ruddy face, punctuated with gray eyes, betrayed his love for the bottle.

He entered the breakfast mess and scowled because a young crew member, William S. Lewis, finished his meal before he yielded his place at the table to the new captain.

After breakfast, Cannon ordered Lewis to bring him a yawl to go ashore. He reprimanded Lewis when the young man had a subordinate fetch the yawl.

"I ordered you, sir, to do it."

"And I order Jimmy to do it," replied Lewis defiantly.

Captain Cannon later ordered Lewis and Lieutenant Butler, the ship's second in command, to give up their bunks, which had been bought and paid for by Lewis, to other crew members—an order that Lewis and even Butler refused to obey.

Cannon had alienated at least part of his crew before the voyage ever began.

A "Yankee miscreant," Lewis called the captain half a century later.

The *Lively* put to sea on November 22 or 23, under threatening skies, with twenty-seven or twenty-eight crew members and passengers, all men, on board.

She had embarked on a voyage in which she would appear and disappear like an apparition of the sea for the next two or three months.

Captain Cannon sailed the *Lively* out of New Orleans and across Lake Pontchartrain, taking her through the Rigolets, the narrow passageway that connected the lake to the Gulf.

She passed on her starboard side the rising curved waterside wall and the bastions and moats of Fort Pike, then being constructed under

President James Monroe's administration, to protect the Rigolets from foreign invasion.

As she reached open sea, according to an account written by Lewis years after the voyage, a powerful gale greeted the *Lively*. It drove the little vessel straight eastward, directly away from her destination, for thirty-six hours. Under Cannon, the crew believed the storm may have taken them clear to the Bahama Islands, off the southeast coast of Florida, at some 750 miles, an improbable distance.

Obviously, Cannon had lost his bearings.

The gale died. The *Lively* became becalmed, her sails hanging listless, according to Lewis. She rose and fell on glassy swells, drifting for a day and a half. The winds then came again out of the west, followed by a second gale, which battered the ship once more. "The poor devils of immigrants," Lewis called the passengers.

Finally the weather changed. Winds grew favorable. Cannon could turn the *Lively* to the west. After some four weeks, by now late in December, he found the mouth of the Sabine River, the border with Mexico. At last he knew his location.

Cannon sailed the *Lively* on a good east wind past the entrance to Galveston Bay, said Lewis. The captain brought her about and beat back into the wind, to the east, sailing the *Lively* into Galveston Bay, where, to his surprise, he discovered at anchor another schooner, about the same size as the *Lively*. Cannon dropped his anchor just to the west of the second vessel.

Lieutenant Butler took a yawl alongside the other ship and learned from her crew that she was a privateer that preyed, under command of a Captain Roach, on Mexican shipping in the Gulf. With the *Lively* anchored not one hundred yards away, Roach and his buccaneers weighed anchor and sailed their little schooner out of Galveston Bay in the middle of the night, disappearing like a shadow in a blackened room.

The *Lively* lay at anchor, Lewis wrote, its crew and passengers fishing, hunting, and reprovisioning the vessel. One party netted so many fish that it could not raise the seine from the water. Another party killed a large black bear, two turkeys and a rabbit.

After several days, near the end of 1821, Captain Cannon ordered his crew to weigh anchor and unfurl sails. He sailed the *Lively* out of Galveston Bay and turned westward, into heavy wind and intermittent rain. When he reached the mouth of the Brazos River—not the Colorado River, the designated rendezvous with Austin—he turned toward shore. He may have believed he had reached the mouth of the Colorado. He may simply have been eager to rid himself of the immigrants. He worked his way through the sandbars to reach a landing.

He discharged the immigrants and the cargo, presumably including Austin's trunks with the gifts for Governor Martinez, onto the sands of the west bank of the Brazos. He left Austin's colonists to fend for themselves, probably thankful to be done with Cannon's captaincy and their unexpectedly long voyage, but uncertain and anxious about their new location.

Cannon returned to the Gulf. The immigrants thought that he might turn the *Lively* westward once more. Some believed that he sailed for Matamoros, on the western side of the mouth of the Rio Grande, to seek another cargo to transport back to New Orleans. Others, concerned about where they had come ashore, hoped that he would verify the location of the mouth of the Colorado River and somehow notify Austin. All hoped that he would return and report. Most never saw Captain Cannon or the *Lively* again.

Concerned about their need for food and shelter and an approaching planting season, the immigrants made their way upstream and set about carving new homes out of the wilderness.

That was the story of the *Lively* according to Lewis.

Strangely, the story according to Edward Lovelace and his brother—both immigrant passengers on the *Lively*—was very different.

Lovelace said nothing at all of the tremendous gales and becalming described by Lewis. He said nothing about Galveston Bay or a pirate ship. He claimed that Captain Cannon sailed the *Lively* past the mouth of the Brazos on the third of December, eleven or twelve days after the departure from New Orleans (a date when Lewis's story had the ship in the far eastern part of the Gulf of Mexico). According to Lovelace, Cannon returned to the Brazos to land the immigrants and cargo, leaving them to their fate on the western bank of the river's mouth on December 23.

Lovelace gives no account of what had happened during the period between December 3 and December 23. It was as though the *Lively* simply disappeared in early December and reappeared just before Christmas.

In both Lewis's and Lovelace's versions, none of the immigrants appears to have had any real notion of where Cannon took the *Lively* after he deposited them at the mouth of the Brazos. The only thing they could say with certainty was that he simply vanished into the Gulf of Mexico.

Cannon's disappearance seems a fitting end to his inexplicably prolonged and circuitous voyage in the Gulf and his landing at the wrong river mouth.

In January 1822, Austin completed his overland journey from Nacogdoches and reached the mouth of the Colorado, where he expected to find the immigrants who had sailed on the *Lively*. He searched fruitlessly for

74

them for two months, growing increasingly worried.

Rumors spread among other immigrants who settled in the lands of Austin's colony. The *Lively*, said one, foundered on a sandbar, with all aboard being lost. The immigrants, said another rumor, reached shore, only to be attacked and murdered by Indians, or they reached shore, where starvation took some and Karankawas rescued others. Captain Cannon, said yet another rumor, commandeered the *Lively* and turned her to piracy.

Austin, by now profoundly concerned, returned to San Antonio in early March. The *Lively* and her passengers and cargo, even his trunks with "the little presents to our friends," appeared to be lost. He then learned, to his shock, that Governor Martinez's confirmation of his inheritance of the colonization grants had been rejected by higher authorities in Monterrey. Austin would have to travel clear to Mexico City to try to resolve the problem.

He left with grave anxieties, believing that the *Lively* may have foundered, with all passengers and cargo lost. He feared that his grant might be rendered invalid, placing at risk the good-faith claims of those immigrants who were already staking out new homes and new lives in Texas. His entire colonization effort now stood in jeopardy, even as thousands more immigrants in the United States prepared to depart for Austin's grant and a new life.

Meanwhile, even as Austin searched the lower Colorado for the immigrants, the *Lively*, in fact, nestled snugly in her berth in New Orleans. Apparently without bothering to get word to anyone—including, in particular, Stephen F. Austin in Texas—Captain Cannon and his crew had simply sailed the *Lively* back to New Orleans, arriving sometime in January or early February.

Within months, Cannon again sailed the *Lively* out of Lake Pontchartrain, through the Rigolets, and into the open sea, carrying immigrants and supplies to Texas. Again, the *Lively* promptly disappeared. Again, rumors promptly arose.

Cannon sailed her to Matamoros and sold the ship and the cargo, said one rumor. She foundered on the coast in a storm, with all aboard being lost, said another.

The last rumor, at least, held some element of truth.

According to Thomas M. Duke, an immigrant aboard the *Lively* during the second voyage, Captain Cannon managed to run the little ship aground on the western end of Galveston Island, near San Luis Pass. Another schooner, the *John Motley,* which happened to be nearby, rescued crew and passengers. The sea took the cargo. The *Lively* broke up, presumably under the pounding of heavy breakers, and vanished for the last time.

Her immigrants fared little better. Under the hardships of the Texas frontier, nearly all of them eventually drifted back east, across the Sabine River, into the United States once more. They, like Captain Cannon, faded from Texas history.

Postscript
The Brazoria County Historical Museum, located in Angleton, fifteen to twenty miles north of where Cannon landed the immigrants on the Brazos River at the end of December in 1821, offers a nationally recognized exhibit on the colonial period of Texas history. Sixty-eight panels provide a chronology of the events from the earliest Anglo-American penetration to full Texas independence. It also includes a detailed model of the good ship *Lively*.

The Spirits of Goliad

As far as I can discover, the spirits of Presidio La Bahía in Goliad recall the pageantry of early Texas history more vividly than those of any other region in the state.

There we will discover, they say, the apparitions of grieving Spanish mothers, shrouded women, Franciscan priests, and dueling swordsmen. We will feel the air chill suddenly as they pass us by.

We will hear the thudding footsteps of an unknown and invisible figure, infants' cries from unmarked graves, chanting voices from vacant mission chapel pews, choruses from empty mission chapel choir lofts, muted organ notes played by unseen hands, and the groans and screams of massacred and long-buried Texas soldiers.

The spiritual sights and sounds of Goliad echo a century and a half of historical forces that, in hindsight, seem to have flowed like tributaries to a swift river and a waiting sea. The cast of characters—La Salle, de León, Manzanet, Mother María, Austin, Houston, Fannin, Travis, Bowie, Crockett, Santa Anna, Cos, Urrea, the Apaches, the Comanches, the Coahuiltecans, the Caddos—seems to have marched across a panoramic stage, enacting scripted roles, to their appointed destinies, into legend.

They seasoned the story with the perpetual human themes of heroism and villainy, honor and treachery, valor and cowardice, brilliance and foolishness, commitment and indecisiveness, nobility and meanness, patriotism and betrayal. Bold and restless adventurers, they defined the heart of Texas.

The spirits of Goliad whisper to us, voices from the past, reminding us of our roots and our heritage.

• • •

On April 22, 1689, a party of Spaniards, including Captain Alonso de León, Father Damian Manzanet, two Indian guides, a French refugee and twenty-five soldiers marched up a light-colored sandy rise overlooking Garcitas Creek, not far above its juncture with the northwestern turn of Lavaca Bay. About forty-five miles east of where Goliad stands today, they found a grim and macabre scene—the desolate, shattered remains of Texas' first colony, Fort St. Louis, the name chosen by Robert Cavalier, the Sieur de la Salle, to honor Louis XIV, France's fabled Sun King.

Louis XIV might have wondered at the homage paid him at this humble site on the Texas coast, since he was at the time in the midst of constructing his magnificent château at Versailles, thirty miles west of Paris.

"We arrived at about eleven in the forenoon," Manzanet reported later to his church superiors and the Spanish authorities, "and found six houses, not very large, built with poles plastered with mud, and roofed over with buffalo hides, another larger house where pigs were fattened, and a wooden fort made from the hulk of a wrecked vessel."

Karankawa Indians had struck La Salle's Fort St. Louis two months earlier, sacking the compound.

"There was a great lot of shattered weapons, broken by the Indians—firelocks, carabines, cutlasses—but they had not left the cannon, only one being found," said Manzanet. "We found two unburied bodies, which I interred, setting up a cross over the grave. There were many torn-up books, and many dead pigs."

The Spaniards speculated that the Indians may have thrown other bodies of French settlers into Garcitas Creek, where they became a meal for the numerous alligators.

La Salle could hardly have foreseen that he would be the first character to appear in the drama of the colonization of Texas, that he and his country, France, would be regarded by Spain as a threat to its claim to the land, that his fledgling settlement would be recalled in the later history of colonialism and revolution at Goliad.

La Salle had intended to settle not at Lavaca Bay but at the mouth of the Mississippi River, some 450 miles to the east. He had explored that great stream from Canada to the Gulf of Mexico in 1681 and 1682, staking France's claim to the entire Mississippi River drainage basin. Returning to France, he quickly won Louis XIV's authorization and financial support to colonize Louisiana.

He departed La Rochelle, on the Atlantic coast of France, 240 miles southwest of Paris, in the summer of 1684, with a squadron of four ships transporting settlers, soldiers, missionaries and crew—more than three hundred altogether—and farming equipment, tools, provisions, weaponry and munitions, the stuff of colonization.

The expedition encountered trouble at the outset. With their responsibilities and authorities poorly defined by French maritime officials, La Salle and the squadron's commander, Beaujeu, quarreled incessantly, disputing everything from ships' anchorages to the soldiers' charge.

The ships became separated during foul weather in the Caribbean. The *St. Francis,* the vessel carrying the colonists' critically needed munitions as well as other cargo, fell into the hands of Spanish buccaneers near Hispaniola. The pirates alerted Spain to La Salle's pending settlement.

After the remaining three vessels—including the *Amiable*, laden with cargo; the *Joli*, a thirty-six-gun frigate; and the *Belle*, a gift from Louis XIV to La Salle—rejoined and passed through the islands of the Caribbean Sea, they overshot the mouth of the Mississippi. (The low-lying northern Gulf coast, with its lack of landmarks and confusion of currents, had long raised difficult navigation problems.)

Not until La Salle and Beaujeu saw the Gulf coastline trending southward did they realize that they must have passed the Mississippi and approached the border of Mexico. La Salle proposed returning eastward along the coast, back toward the mouth of the river. Beaujeu agreed, but he wanted more of the expedition's provisions for the *Joli* than La Salle was prepared to give up. The two feuded to a standoff.

Rather than compromise, La Salle headed his immigrants into Matagorda Bay, up into Lavaca Bay, and staked his colony on the Texas Gulf coast. It was now February 1686.

The commander of the *Amiable*, with its vital cargo of supplies and provisions for the colony, promptly ran his ship aground just outside the pass where he tried to sail into Matagorda Bay. He lost the vessel and most of its cargo.

Even as La Salle explored his new home, Beaujeu summarily sailed away for France, leaving the colony on the wild Texas coast on March 12, 1686. He took the *Amiable* crew. He took all the cannonballs, rendering La Salle's artillery essentially useless.

Deserted and isolated, La Salle's colony now faced impossible odds.

To make things even worse, the crew of the fifty-one-foot, two-masted *Belle* became decimated by fatal accidents and disease and, shorthanded in a storm, the sailors lost control of their vessel. She ran aground in the southwestern corner of Matagorda Bay, near the point where Port O'Connor stands today. This cut off any chance for the settlers to escape by sea.

On the rise on the western bank of Garcitas Creek, the settlers cobbled together a village, including fortifications fashioned from hull timbers salvaged from the *Amiable*. They began what would become a hopeless struggle for survival.

Indians ambushed and mutilated scouting parties. Disease laid a heavy hand on the colony. The settlers quarreled among themselves. Colonist murdered colonist. Mutiny brewed.

La Salle, desperate, led twenty men in an overland bid to seek relief from French settlements in Illinois, a thousand miles across wilderness. He failed when ammunition essential for hunting ran short. He turned back for Fort St. Louis, arriving in October 1686, with only eight of his men having survived the hardships of the trail.

Three months later, La Salle began another attempt to reach Illinois. Somewhere in East Texas on March 20, one of the party, a man named Duhaut, ambushed and shot La Salle to death. A priest buried La Salle, erecting a cross over his grave at a location now lost to history. Survivors again returned to Fort St. Louis and to more quarreling, more murders, and desertions.

At that point the Karankawas, appalled by the behavior of the settlers, put an end to La Salle's colonization cancer. They struck Fort St. Louis and killed all the colonists present except for a few children, whom they took as prisoners. They reduced the site to the shambles found by de León and Manzanet two months later.

The Spaniards had come to assess the French threat to their claim to Texas. They had their answer. They turned west toward Mexico and home.

They would not, however, forget Fort St. Louis and its location on a rise above Garcitas Creek, not far from where it discharged its waters into Lavaca Bay.

• • •

Those stars of history that change the course of events in human affairs now seemed to fall into conjunction.

Although it failed, La Salle's settlement alarmed the Spaniards about the danger of French encroachment in the long neglected northeastern frontier.

Spain, its economy plummeting like a star falling into a black hole, had become paranoid about any perceived threats to its grandiose territorial pretensions. (The Spanish monarchy had laid claim to the entire Gulf of Mexico and the coastal lands, insisting that the entire region was off limits to any other nation. Spain simply lacked the ability to enforce the claim.)

Spain's influential clergy, an expression of the nation's religious fervor and mysticism, felt driven to gather conversions to Roman Catholicism.

The Franciscans were eager to question the Indians about claims by the "Lady in Blue"—Mother María Jesús of Agreda, a nun of Saint Francis's Poor Clares—that her spirit had "flown" from northern Spain by teleportation hundreds of times earlier in the century to minister to the tribes of Texas.

The Indians, especially the Jumanos and the Tejas tribes, clamored for Spanish missions.

The time seemed to be right.

Spain decided on a strategy to strengthen its hold on Texas. Much as it had done in the Southwest and northern Mexico, Spain would build missions to convert the Indians, settlements to put down roots, and presidios to provide law enforcement and protection.

The first colonizing expeditions arrived in 1690, the year after de León and Manzanet found the remains of the French debacle at Fort St. Louis on Garcitas Creek. The Spaniards built their first missions and settlements in East Texas, where they hoped to counter emerging French influence from Louisiana. The colonies faltered, however, and within a few years the Spanish abandoned the area. Spanish colonization in Texas sputtered for more than two decades.

In 1716, prodded by further French incursions, Spain resumed her effort to colonize Texas and to convert the Indians to Christianity, in East Texas and along the San Antonio River.

Unknowingly, Spain had entered a long, dark period of frontier hardship and conflict, a breeding ground for those fleeting and ephemeral spirits that still haunt Presidio La Bahía centuries later.

• • •

Marques de San Miguel de Aguayo, a wealthy Spanish nobleman of Coahuila and the governor of Coahuila and Texas from October 1719 through May 1722, founded the Presidio Nuestra Señora de Loreto and the Mission Espíritu Santo de Zúñiga—known together as "La Bahía"—in April of 1722 (in English, the term means, simply "the Bay").

He built the presidio with its own chapel to stand, symbolically, on the ruins of La Salle's Fort St. Louis, on the rise overlooking Garcitas Creek.

The mission was constructed nearby, across Garcitas Creek.

The monarchy charged La Bahía, with its garrison of a mere ninety soldiers under the command of José Domingo Ramon, with protecting the entire Texas Gulf coast from incursions by the French.

The church charged the mission's Franciscan priests with Christianizing the coastal tribes of the Karankawas, Cujanes, and Cocos, who had already seen, and perhaps contributed to, the French calamity.

Under Commander Ramón, La Bahía's military garrison not only failed to guard the coast, it failed to protect La Bahía. It sank into a cesspool of sadistic cruelty and degeneracy. Officers and soldiers abused the Indians and raped the women. Many drank themselves into oblivion and gambled away their pay. They neglected the post's defenses. They used palisade timbers for firewood, not defense. As a result, La Bahía suffered relentless Indian raids, livestock losses, and casualties.

The friars became disgusted, the Indians, incensed. Hostilities arose.

The tinderbox ignited over a simple incident. One of the Indian neophytes, waiting for a ration of beef, shook the dust from his blanket. The cloud settled on corn being ground by an officer's wife. The woman, enraged, screamed for her husband to flog the Indian. The situation escalated into a fight. The Indian sliced the officer with a knife.

Soldiers grabbed the Indian. They meant to kill him, but some forty Indian men struck back with bows and arrows, wounding a number of Spanish soldiers.

The Indians took their families and possessions and fled La Bahía for the wilderness.

The garrison notified Commander Ramón, who, with a troop of soldiers, quickly ran down the Indians.

"Come back," he told them unctuously. "Lay down your bows and arrows. No one will be punished."

The Indians believed him. They had been taught, after all, that Christians forgive.

Ramón drew them back into the presidio—and promptly crowded them all into a post hut and imprisoned them.

He tried to call them out one at a time, saying that he would reprimand each one individually, then hand out a ration of beef.

The Indians could see the soldiers constructing gallows and refused to leave their prison. Ramón entered the hut. Hissing like the snake in the Garden of Eden, he tried to soothe the Indians' fears. Then he screamed to his men, "At them, kill them!"

The soldiers poured gunfire into the hut. Many Indians died. A few escaped. One, a young woman, fell captive to the soldiers.

In the melee, a Karankawa warrior stabbed Ramón with a scissors blade. The wound did not temper Ramón's venomous cruelty. He had the captured young woman hung.

A few days later, Ramón died.

• • •

The Spanish military and Franciscan friars moved La Bahía—the presidio with its chapel and the mission—from La Salle's Fort St. Louis site, and its dark history, to Mission Valley on the Guadalupe River, on the Gulf coast prairieland a few miles upstream from today's Victoria, in 1726.

La Bahía began to prosper, like a plant that has escaped a deep shade and found the sunlight. The friars converted more than four hundred Aranama Indians. The mission built an extensive irrigation system. It produced substantial crops. It ran thousands of head of Longhorns, mustangs, and sheep on more than a million acres of rangeland. It celebrated fiestas with parades, dances, mock duels, rodeos, and bullfighting. Although it had intermittent problems with its Indian population, La Bahía had become, after nearly a quarter of a century, one of the most successful Spanish colonies in Texas.

So the Spaniards decided to move La Bahía yet again.

• • •

Under the direction of Dr. Mardith K. Schuetz, an authority on the Spanish mission period, the Texas Archaeological Society excavated the second La Bahía presidio site, just east of the Guadalupe River, in the late 1960's.

It lay on the bank of an oxbow cutoff, near a limestone deposit that had served the Spanish as a quarry for building stone. A wagon road, still discernible, led the few hundred yards from the quarry to the site where the presidio stood. Excavation of the foundation revealed little more than a jumble of stone, although the archaeologists did find what may have been the base of the belfry tower for the presidio's chapel. More recent farmers had probably reused much of the presidio building stone to construct their own homes and barns. Their fields overlay most of the presidio's irrigation system.

Excavation in the presidio cemetery led to the discovery of a burial that, as far as I know, remains unexplained to this day. As they removed the overlying soil, the archaeologists thought at first that the skeletal material might be that of an Indian; the remains might reveal something of mission Indian burial practices, maybe even something of mission Indian health.

They found, however, that the skeleton belonged not to an Indian but to an Anglo-Saxon, a man dressed in a uniform at the time of his burial. Encrusted brass buttons lay beside the long bones of the legs.

The archaeologists reburied the skeleton where it lay, but they recovered one button and took it to an archaeology laboratory, where they cleaned away its crust. Remarkably, they could then read the letters imprinted in the metal: "TEXAS NAVY."

The Texas Navy, created by the Texas Council in November 1835, early in the Texas Revolution, consisted of four sailing vessels, the *Liberty*, the *Independence*, the *Brutus*, and the *Invincible*. During its existence, it harassed Mexican shipping trying to resupply Santa Anna's Mexican army in Texas. It threatened Mexican marine commerce to gain leverage in negotiations to force Mexican recognition of the Republic of Texas. It reinforced Texas claims of sovereignty by flying the flag on the high seas. It passed intact into the navy of the United States when Texas attained statehood in 1845.

We will probably never know how someone who was, presumably, a veteran of the Texas Navy, which existed only a decade, came to be buried in the cemetery of the presidio on the Guadalupe River a century after the Spanish moved La Bahía to its third and final home.

• • •

José de Escandon y Elguera, colonizer and governor of a proposed province that would extend from Matagorda Bay to Tampico, moved the La Bahía mission and presidio from the Guadalupe River to the San Antonio River, where Goliad stands today, in 1749. He aimed to reorganize the settlements and, at last, to pacify and convert the Karankawas.

Here, the Spaniards, threatened by the Apaches and Comanches from the north and west and by the coastal tribes from the south, raised a powerful bastion for defense.

At the crest of a low hill overlooking the river, they constructed the new Presidio La Bahía of heavy wooden beams and river rock, encompassing a three-acre plaza. They maintained a garrison of eighty soldiers. They fortified the presidio with eight-pounder cannon and swivel guns. Within the fortress walls, they built a new chapel, personnel quarters, and other facilities.

Across the river northwest from the presidio, the Spaniards erected the new Espiritú Santo de Zúñiga mission, including the church, the missionary housing, and the work quarters. They enclosed the mission with a stockade.

The Franciscans felt so optimistic about the future of their new home in Goliad that they founded a new mission, Nuestra Señora del Rosario, primarily for the Karankawas, in 1754. They constructed it four miles west of the presidio. The missionaries and Indian converts raised a new church, living quarters, and a granary.

Under the protective umbrella of the presidio, the Franciscan priests at the two missions set out to convince ancient peoples of the Texas wilderness of the superiority and desirability of the modern Spanish vision of life, values, and religion.

They faced a difficult job.

The Indians had long ago found ways to take their living from the wilderness. Clams, oysters, turtles, and fish from the bays and estuaries of the Gulf. Buffalo, antelope, bear, deer, peccary, and rabbit from the rolling prairies. Cattail roots, water chinquapin, pecans, blackberries, prickly pear fruit, mesquite beans, and grains from lagoons and the land.

The Indians built housing of slender willow poles covered with mats and skins. They wove baskets, manufactured pottery, produced dugout canoes. They made clothing from animal skins. The men, exceptionally tall and muscular, fashioned bows that could drive arrows completely through an adult bear (provided you were strong enough to pull the bow).

These nomads wandered in small bands, or extended families, at will across the Gulf coast prairies and marshes, claiming their living where they could find it, with the concept of individual land ownership being beyond their grasp.

The men took their wives always from other bands to avoid incest, and they avoided in-laws like they might avoid the plague. Wives joined the men's bands. Should no children be born, the men felt free to buy, sell, swap, and loan wives, increasing chances for reproduction. The bands doted on the children, the future of the tribe.

Like other hunting and gathering peoples, the Indians of the Texas Gulf coastal area probably led a profoundly spiritual life, with the earth and sky serving as their temple. They vested all the natural things with spiritual presence and life. They danced to celebrate their successes in hunting or fishing, to pray to their deities for future successes, and to mourn the deaths of relatives and friends. They called on their shamans to connect them to the spirit world and to heal their illnesses and their wounds.

The coastal Indians held great pride in themselves as a people. In spite of the hardships of surviving the wilderness and their fear of tribes from the north, they revered the way they lived.

The Franciscan priest, light of skin, sandled, dressed in a blue or gray robe bound at the waist with a rope tie, usually unable to string, much less draw, a Karankawa bow, now appeared, uninvited, from the south and the west to redirect ways of life that had evolved over centuries.

His "medicine," from the Indian point of view, appeared to be the rosary beads and cross that hung from his waist.

The Franciscan learned the tribal language and told the Indians—those he could attract (or shanghai) to the mission—that they must give up foraging, fishing, and hunting and must turn to breaking the soil, cultivating fields, and harvesting cotton, potatoes, and beans. They must plant orchards, raise trees, and pick apples, pears, and peaches.

They must give up the freedom of the nomadic life and instead take up residence in a permanent community and learn the value of property. They must live in rooms made of stone, learn to be herdsmen, weavers, blacksmiths. The men must marry but one woman, for life, in a ceremony performed at the altar in a church. For better or for worse. Children or no children.

They must give up dancing in joy, sorrow, or prayer before their deities of antiquity, give up shamanistic visits to the world of their spirits. They must learn new ceremonies and rituals and worship a single god, who had a galaxy of saints who wore long robes and had white faces. They must gather early in the morning in the pews of the church to pray, receive instruction and chant Old Testament verses. They must then work in the fields, the orchards, and the shops. They must return to the church in the afternoon, men, women, and children, to learn the catechisms, the principles of the church. They must reassemble again at the church in the evening to hear instruction, pray, and sing hymns. When they retire to their homes, they must recite prayers and recite hymns until far into the night.

Should mission Indians—*reducidos,* the "reduced," they were called—attempt to escape, soldiers tried to run them down. Those they could catch, they hauled back to the mission, where they whipped and punished the runaways.

Meanwhile, Apaches, Comanches, and other tribes raided the missions again and again, killing Spaniards and *reducidos* alike, plundering the stores, stealing and killing the livestock.

Many neophytes simply abandoned mission life, returning to the wilderness, "irreducible."

• • •

Once, many years ago, I visited with a young Franciscan priest at San Antonio's San Juan Capistrano Mission, which serves poor Latino neighborhoods. Born in Cincinnati, he had somewhere learned to speak the beautiful Spanish of Castilla.

"One of these days, when I get time," he said, "I am going to research the archives at the archdiocese to see if I can learn why the Indians left the missions."

"Father," I said, "the old padres effectively enslaved and beat a people who had been wild and free."

"Yes," he replied, "but look what we gave them: Christianity and civilization."

The wonder is not that the missionary effort in Texas failed but that it lasted as long as it did.

• • •

The Franciscans did experience some success, albeit hard won, in New Mexico, where Pueblo tribes traditionally lived in settled villages, worked in fields, and worshiped in central places. Mission churches still stand as places of worship at Acoma, Laguna, Taos, Ysleta, and other pueblos.

The fathers found much less success in Texas, where tribes drifted with the seasons, took their living from hunting, fishing, foraging, and raiding, and worshiped at movable campfires.

By the late eighteenth century and early nineteenth century, the forces that energized the Spanish colonization and Christianization of Texas had dissipated. New stars of history had come into alignment. The course of events in Texas was about to change again.

Mexico lurched toward revolt. Spain warred with France in Europe. The Comanches and Apaches raided frontier settlements remorselessly. The Franciscan missionaries gave up hope for further Christianization of Texas Indians. They began turning over mission facilities and land to local authorities. Settlers drifted from Texas back to Mexico. Most dramatically, the new colossus to the east, having broken its English bonds, strained at its western boundaries. Its people yearned for new frontiers to explore, new lands to exploit. American mercenaries moved into Texas to join forces with revolutionaries and drive Spanish forces from the land, intending, ultimately, to join it to the United States.

La Bahía was about to become the scene of some of the most pivotal events in not one major revolution but two!

• • •

In the fall of 1812, under the command of Colonel Augustus William Magee, a graduate of West Point, a combined American and Mexican revolutionary, or Republican, force of about 800 troops drove Spanish, or Royalist, forces from La Bahía presidio and occupied the fortress. Three days later, a Royalist force of about 1,500 troops, under the command of Manuel María de Salcedo, counterattacked, assaulting the fort. The Republicans drove them back. The Royalists laid siege, received reinforcements, then assaulted the fort three more times. The Republicans drove them back each time.

At that point, Magee apparently lost his nerve. In council with Salcedo, Magee agreed to surrender the presidio. He announced his decision to his officers and men, who unanimously rejected Magee's unilateral action, angrily slamming their rifle butts onto the ground to make their point.

When the Republicans refused to honor Magee's agreement, Salcedo attacked the presidio. The rebels, under a new commander, Major Samuel Kemper, drove the Royalists from the fortress walls, inflicting some two hundred casualties while suffering minimal losses. The battle ended at sundown.

Magee had withdrawn to his quarters, where he hovered throughout the fighting. The Republicans found him dead sometime after midnight, a victim, many believed, of suicide or, possibly, murder.

The Royalist forces held the siege until March 1813, when Salcedo ordered his men to give up the struggle, abandon their positions, and return to San Antonio.

The Republicans, now tested on the anvil of battle at La Bahía, found themselves reinforced by Americans, Indians, Royalist deserters, and Texas settlers. Under Kemper, the rebels left the presidio, ran down Salcedo's Royalists, and destroyed the Spanish force at the juncture of the San Antonio and Salado Rivers. Not long after, the Royalists won back lost territory and reoccupied Presidio La Bahía.

• • •

In the spring of 1817, Colonel Henry Perry, a veteran of the campaign under Magee and Kemper, led a Republican force of only fifty men to attack Presidio La Bahía and demanded that the Royalists surrender the fortress. Royalist forces surprised Perry, about nine miles east of the presidio, attacking him from the rear. The Royalists from the presidio poured out to strike him head on. Seeing the imminent annihilation of his men, Perry turned his pistol on himself and blew out his brains.

• • •

When the ragtag Texas army of General Sam Houston overran and destroyed the veteran Mexican regular army of General Santa Anna, the

"Napoleon of the West," on the banks of the San Jacinto River and Buffalo Bayou on the afternoon of April 21, 1836, the battle cries of "Remember the Alamo" and "Remember Goliad" rose above the melody of a fife, the beat of a drum, the crack of the musket, the thunder of cannon, the screams and pleas of a quickly beaten enemy.

"Remember the Alamo" symbolized what the Texans fought for: the inalienable rights of the individual; the freedom, dignity and nobility of the human soul; the heroism of those would give their lives for an idea. "Remember Goliad" signified what the Texans fought against: the disregard of individual rights, the oppression of a people, the arrogant tyranny and malevolent treachery of a self proclaimed emperor.

The Texas Revolution almost appears, uncannily, to have been orchestrated by some greater hand, one that guided men and events to a predetermined conclusion. It wove a kind of magic that drew men who saw a cause and adventure as more important than life.

The 182 men who defended the walls of the Alamo against Santa Anna's overwhelming forces seemed bound by destiny and legend in the making. They marched to the Alamo prepared to die in the name of a principle, for the notions of honor and courage. The commander, William B. Travis, gave fervor and noble voice to their ideals. James Bowie and David Crockett, larger than life, validated their purpose. Men who could have escaped competed for the honor of defending the most dangerous ramparts. Men fought their way into the Alamo, there to show that they cared and to give their lives. In those terrible days between February 23 and March 6, 1836, the 182 men in the Alamo killed and wounded more than 2,000 Mexican soldiers, more than ten of the enemy for every defender, destroying more than a third of Santa Anna's immediate command. They became known in Mexican fable as the *diablos tejanos,* the "devil Texans."

By contrast, the men at Goliad who defended the walls of the old Spanish Presidio La Bahía against the onrushing forces under Santa Anna's general José Urrea could sense calamity in the making. Under a failing leadership, they thought more of escape than of principle. When attacked, their leader tried to bargain with the devil. They paid with their lives.

Remember the Alamo! Remember Goliad!

Houston won the independence of Texas and changed the course of Western history in less than an hour on the plain at San Jacinto.

• • •

Mid-March, 1836.
James W. Fannin, commander of La Bahía's 500 men, struggled, not

to prepare his men for the coming battle, but to control the paralysis inflicted by his own fears and indecision. He felt the terror a matador feels when he has lost his nerve and cannot plant his feet as the bull passes and the crowd boos him to humiliate him for his cowardice.

Fannin knew that General Urrea, a superb field commander with some 1,700 to 1,800 professional soldiers, had crossed the Rio Grande at Matamoros and now marched up the great crescent of the Texas Gulf coast to engage him in battle.

He knew that he had failed to answer the call by Travis to reinforce the gallant men at the Alamo.

He knew that the Alamo had fallen.

He knew that he had failed to act on Sam Houston's direct order to blast the Presidio La Bahía walls to rubble, and he knew that he had failed to lead his desperately needed forces, the largest in Texas at the moment, from Goliad to join the general in his march toward San Jacinto and the ultimate battle with Santa Anna.

He knew that the meager Texas forces that had foolishly dreamed of crossing the Rio Grande and attacking Matamoros had been decimated by Urrea near San Patricio.

He knew that men he sent to Refugio to warn Texas civilians to withdraw had met their doom at the hands of Urrea. Their bodies lay on the earth, awaiting the coyotes and wolves.

He knew that Urrea drew near. The two forces had already skirmished.

Fannin had to make a decision. Stand and fight. Or retreat.

Fannin chose to retreat, to abandon the protection provided by the fortress walls.

He led his men, the some three hundred who remained, northeastward out of Goliad on the morning of March 19 under cover of fog.

The fog lifted. The day turned warm and humid. Within six to eight miles, out in an open prairie, teams of oxen began to falter under heavy loads of cannon and freight.

Fannin ordered a halt. The animals had to have rest.

Not here, implored some of his officers. Push on for another five miles, until we reach the wooded Coleto Creek and water. But Fannin obeyed some inner voice that instructed him to pause on the open prairie, short of water, short of cover.

His inner voice betrayed him. Urrea trapped Fannin on the open plain, cutting the Texans off from Coleto Creek. Mexican cavalry and infantry emerged from timber as if they were apparitions, first by twos and fours, then by the hundreds, forcing Fannin to throw up his defenses in a shallow basin.

From one o'clock in the afternoon into the evening, cannon rumbled. Rifles cracked. Man and animal fell. Fannin took a bullet in the thigh. As night closed in, the gunfire slackened and grew silent. Fannin's cannons had failed in any event, for want of water to cool the barrels. Through the hours of darkness, he could hear his wounded men moaning in pain and crying for water.

The Texans had inflicted as many as four hundred casualties on Urrea's men, but at six-thirty the next morning, March 20, five hundred fresh Mexican soldiers with three cannon arrived from San Antonio to reinforce Urrea and join the battle.

Fannin, hoping to relieve suffering and save lives, ran up a white flag and surrendered, with assurances from Urrea that the Mexicans would ship the Texans back to the United States as soon as possible. General Urrea, an honorable man, meant to keep his promise, believing that the Mexican government would not execute prisoners who appealed for clemency.

He could scarcely have anticipated the actions of Santa Anna, who had other ideas.

Urrea herded Fannin's force, including the wounded, back across the trail to Goliad. The Mexicans packed Fannin's men as well as prisoners taken in earlier engagements—well over four hundred men—into the fortress chapel. Urrea called out Fannin's medical personnel to tend to Mexican casualties.

The prisoners suffered from wretched food and overcrowding, but they believed they would soon move to the coast to board a ship that would take them home. They could endure.

By Saturday, March 26, the day before Palm Sunday that year, the prisoners idled away the time, waiting. Fannin had just returned from the coast with the news that no vessel was immediately available to take them home. They would have to wait longer than they had hoped. Still, they could endure. They were returning to the United States. Fannin even entertained friends. Someone began to play a flute, the melancholy strains of "Home Sweet Home" floating through the gloominess of the chapel.

They had no way that dark evening to know that Urrea had just received orders from Santa Anna that countermanded the surrender agreement. Fannin and his men, said Santa Anna, must be shot. Urrea, a professional officer, must obey orders.

Dawn, March 27. Palm Sunday, the day when Christians remember Jesus' celebrated entry into Jerusalem.

Urrea sent one of his officers, Nicolas Portilla, to awaken the prisoners. Urrea could not face the coming horror himself.

Portilla told some of the prisoners that they must change quarters to make room for Santa Anna, who would be arriving soon. He told others that they had to hunt and butcher cattle for food. He told still others that they would march to the coast to board a vessel and go home. He ordered the able-bodied enlisted men to quit the chapel. He divided them into three columns.

He marched one column to the east of the presidio, toward the river, another to the south, another to the west. Guards forced the prisoners to line up and sit on the ground. Executioners began shooting them in the back of the head. Pandemonium erupted. Some prisoners broke and ran for freedom, most of them shot as they fled. Others stood and turned to their enemies, who were then forced to confront their prisoners face to face as they shot them down.

Portilla's men next dragged the wounded from their beds into the presidio plaza and shot them to death.

They next shot Fannin's officers, who died knowing the fate of their men.

Finally, Portilla's men brought Fannin himself before the firing squad.

Some say that, facing death, Fannin at last found his nerve. He calmly gave his watch to the officer commanding the firing squad, requesting that the watch be sent to the Fannin family. He asked that he be allowed to face his executioners, that he be buried in a decent grave.

Others say that, facing death, Fannin begged for mercy where none had been shown to his men.

The Mexicans shot him in the head and threw his body onto the pile of 342 Texas bodies.

• • •

Dillard Cooper escaped. Unharmed. Miraculously.

He swam the San Antonio River and ran for the woods, where he discovered three comrades, two of them wounded. The four hid until nightfall, when they began making their way to the northeast.

From a rise, they looked back toward Presidio La Bahía and Goliad. "We could not at first account for the numerous fires we saw blazing," said Cooper. "We were not long in doubt, for the sickening smell that was borne towards us by the south wind, informed us too well that they were burning the bodies of our companions.

" . . . some of our men were thrown into the flames and burned alive."

March 27, 1836. Palm Sunday came to an end.

• • •

Remember Goliad.

• • •

The violent and tragic history of Goliad has roots in the France of Louis XIV and a Spain of fading grandeur and religious mysticism. It is a history of lost ships, abandoned souls, shattered dreams, cruelty, betrayal, murder, suicide, Comanche and Apache depredation, missionary failure, revolution and massacre. It is a spawning ground for a cast of ghosts who echo the long-past sorrows and agonies of Indian, Frenchman, Spaniard, Mexican, and Anglo.

Residents and visitors tell of seeing candles glowing in the presidio chapel, deep in the night, long after the lights have been turned out. They tell of seeing a tiny friar, dressed in a black robe, floating through the chapel, from corner to corner. They describe a woman, dressed in mourning, grieving and praying before the chapel altar, then disappearing when someone reaches out to comfort her. They speak of faint images of soldiers, dressed in Spanish uniforms, dueling with swords in the presidio plaza; a woman, wearing a white shroud, who floats through the fogs that engulf Mission Espiritú Santo; a headless horseman, who wears a Texas frontiersman's dress, and rides through dark nights at Presidio La Bahía.

Many report seeing along the San Antonio River the apparition of a beautiful weeping Spanish peasant woman, La Llorona, abandoned by her lover, who drowned their three children in the flowing waters, then committed suicide. Her spirit is condemned to search the banks of the river forever for the lost children. Her story has roots in the ancient Indian civilizations of Mexico.

Those who know Presidio La Bahía well whisper of hearing the cries of infants rising from unmarked graves beside the presidio chapel; voices chanting in unknown tongues; organ music, a soprano's song, a women's choir—strange, ethereal, and unfamiliar music—emanating from the air itself.

And in the night sometimes, there are those who speak of hearing muffled voices and moans and cries from the killing fields where Fannin and his men met their doom.

• • •

Remember Goliad.

• • •

Postscript
The site of La Salle's Fort St. Louis and the first La Bahía presidio lies on private land today and is not accessible to visitors, but a large formal granite statue of La Salle stands on the shore of Indianola and looks, perhaps a bit forlornly, across Lavaca Bay. He could almost see the location where, in July 1995 the Texas Historical Commission discovered the wreckage of the *Belle* in twelve feet of water just offshore from Port O'Connor.

The sites of the second La Bahía presidio and mission lie on private land north of Victoria and are not accessible to visitors, but the Texas Archaeological Society has returned there recently to resume investigations of the history of the location.

The site of the third La Bahía presidio, now a national historic landmark in Goliad and administered by the Diocese of the Victoria Catholic Church, stands as the world's finest example of a Spanish frontier fortress. The church still conducts services in the chapel, where Santa Anna's forces imprisoned Fannin and his men until the massacre.

The Mission Espíritu Santo de Zúñiga stands a short drive from the presidio across the San Antonio River, and it is administered as a state historical park by Texas Parks and Wildlife. The mission Nuestra Señora del Rosario, also under the administration of Texas Parks and Wildlife, lies in ruins.

The Fannin Battleground, on the plain five miles west of Coleto Creek and about ten miles east of Goliad, is marked by a stone obelisk monument and is administered as a state historical park by Texas Parks and Wildlife.

The Truth About Sasquatch

SASQUATCH INTERVIEW

A strange telephone call, I'll admit.

"This is Mr. Walker," the voice said, "with the Texas Division of Sasquatch."

"Sasquatch?"

"You know—Sasquatch. Bigfoot. Yeti. The Abominable Snowman. The Skunk Ape. Alma. The Hairy One."

"Oh, that Sasquatch," I said, suspecting something. It must be my old friend Bill "Wild Willie" Hada from back in the Houston days. He used to be pretty hairy.

"I didn't know that Texas had a Bigfoot," I said.

"Texas has a lot of big feet," said my "Mr. Walker."

Wonderful, I thought. I get a real live Sasquatch on the telephone and he thinks he's a stand-up comedian. "What can I do for you?" I asked.

"We want you to interview our Texas Division Chief, Mr. Stomper," he said.

"Interview your chief?" Somehow this did not sound quite like a Bill Hada joke. I said, "Sasquatch have always been shy and reclusive. I'm told that there may be people who think you don't even exist. Why do you want an interview?"

"Chief Stomper will answer that question. Will you interview him?"

"When?" I felt intrigued. I wanted to know whether this was legitimate or just an elaborate gag. I hoped it was legitimate. I have always wanted to know the whole truth about the Sasquatch.

"One week from tonight. Nine-thirty," said Mr. Walker.

He gave me a meeting place. The end of a dirt road in a wooded area in Ellis County, about thirty miles south of Dallas, close to Waxahachie Creek. Sasquatch have been reported in that area.

95

"I'll be there," I said.

After we hung up, I wondered why the Sasquatch had chosen me to interview their chief. I guessed that they must have known my reputation as a journalist. That, and they probably knew that I had interviewed Cheetwah, the guardian spirit of El Paso's Franklin Mountains, and several politicians of West Texas and New Mexico. That would explain it.

I like to go into interviews fully prepared, so I immediately began to bone up on the Sasquatch.

I discovered that investigators have built up a detailed profile. The average adult male Sasquatch stands seven to nine feet tall and weighs five hundred to one thousand pounds. His torso and short neck look massive enough to support a bridge. His arms, thick as a cedar gate post, extend almost to his knees. His foot measures twenty-two inches or longer, more than twice the length of my foot; and his hand width spans almost seven inches, nearly twice my hand width. Black, brown, or gray hair, one to four inches long, covers his entire body, except for his face, hands, and feet. His eyes, dark brown, gleam with intensity.

The Sasquatch eat all the right foods, almost no fat, few sweets. Fresh fruits, fresh vegetables, fresh water lily bulbs (I do not know whether that is fruit or vegetable), fresh fish, an occasional fresh chicken and a few nuts.

No enchiladas and melted cheese, no fried pork chops or bacon, no T-bone steak, no baked potatoes and butter and sour cream, no fettuccine Alfredo, no popcorn and butter, no hot dogs or hamburgers and french fries and milk shakes, no ice cream or chocolate chip cookies or brownies.

Nuts.

A Sasquatch male has such power that he can easily uproot tree stumps, snap eight-inch-diameter saplings, walk through barbed-wire fences and rip up heavy farm structures. According to one report, a Sasquatch, harassed by motorists at the Lake Worth Nature Center in Fort Worth, threw a tire on the rim more than five hundred feet, far greater than the length of a football field. (The motorists scattered like flushed quail and fled the scene.)

A Sasquatch can accelerate like a black-tailed jackrabbit and run and jump like a white-tailed deer. One account claims that a Sasquatch ran beside a car at eighty miles per hour. Somehow that seems far-fetched to me. I cannot imagine how one could run that fast for more than one hundred yards or so.

The Sasquatch have extraordinary character. The most knowledgeable researchers believe that the Sasquatch marry once and remain forever faithful. They keep their population under control; a couple never produces more than one or two offspring. They revere their environment, never abusing or trashing the forests or the mountains or the streams. They seldom get violent and then only if threatened. (Only a few people have been known to threaten a Sasquatch.) I did not find a single reference to the Sasquatch drinking beer, smoking, or chewing tobacco.

The Sasquatch male has only one significant character flaw, as far as I can discover. He likes to fish.

A Sasquatch is so elusive that a Texas Ranger would have a hard time catching him. Even though researchers report that the Sasquatch and their brethren live in essentially every American state, every Canadian province, eastern Asia, the Himalayan Mountains and Europe, scientists do not have a single Sasquatch, dead or alive, complete or partial, to study and analyze. Not even a single indisputable photograph. Sasquatch have been reported by tens of thousands of people, usually at night, most often in remote forested areas. They have left thousands of footprints and even a few samples of handprints and hair tufts. They often leave behind a strange and pungent smell. The Indians of the northwestern United States became so impressed that they believed the Sasquatch could materialize or dematerialize at will, something like Barry Sanders of the Detroit Lions football team.

A week after the telephone call from Mr. Walker, I felt ready to interview the chief, Mr. Stomper. I hoped that this whole thing was not a hoax. I particularly wanted to check out stories I had read about the Sasquatch in Texas, and I wanted to find out why the Sasquatch, after all this time, suddenly wanted to talk to a journalist.

I drove to Ellis County and, as Mr. Walker had instructed, out the dirt road through the woods, each mile taking me further into the night. I soon felt as though I were entering an Egyptian pharaonic tomb, deeper and deeper, chamber by chamber into the darkness. I came to the end of the road. My headlights illuminated an open stand of pecan trees. I thought that I must be close to Waxahachie Creek. I stopped the car, turned off the lights, put a notebook and pencil into my pocket, and stepped out into the blackness.

If this turned out to be Bill Hada's idea of a joke . . .

"Do not turn around." I recognized the voice of Mr. Walker. He stood behind me. I smelled an odd musky odor. "I'm going to blindfold you and take you to Mr. Stomper," he said. I felt a soft cloth cover my eyes.

"A blindfold won't help," I said. "I can't see a thing in this darkness in any event. There's no moon tonight."

"I know," said Mr. Walker. "We planned for that. Now, come with me." I felt his hand take me by my wrist. The palm, strangely soft, extended almost the length of my forearm. He led me, stumbling over roots, through the trees, through the silence of the black forest. I worried about stepping on a copperhead or a diamondback rattler. That could be exasperating.

I tried at first to count the steps and turns. I soon lost all track.

After what seemed like an hour, we stopped. I felt the blindfold taken from my face. A small, cheerful fire illuminated an opening surrounded by a perhaps a dozen trees. "Please have a seat," said Mr. Walker. I heard him disappearing back into the woods. I realized that I stood before a log, its bark polished from long use. I sat on the ground and leaned back against the log.

"Welcome," said a new voice, deep, modulated, sounding like Charlton Heston playing Moses. "I am Mr. Stomper, Texas Division Chief of the Sasquatch." He sat in the shadows, the flickering light barely reaching his form. "Thank you for coming."

In the darkness, I could barely make out Mr. Stomper's bulky silhouette, sitting on the ground, evidently as relaxed as an old cat before a fireplace. I know this is hard to believe, but he was the first Sasquatch I ever saw. He seemed massive, blanketed, as far as I could tell, with dark hair. Nothing like Bill Hada. I could barely see his eyes twinkling in the light of the fire. I detected that strange odor. I had a sense that other Sasquatch watched from the woods, just beyond the reach of the firelight.

"Thank you for having me," I said, feeling a little bit as if I were talking to a shadow. "There are lots of questions I want to ask about the Sasquatch in Texas, and I would like to know why you have requested an interview."

"Let's deal with your questions first," Mr. Stomper said.

"Before this," I said, "I had thought that the Sasquatch all lived up in the Northwest—

Northern California, Idaho, Washington, maybe British Columbia."

"We live all over the place," he replied. "A lot more of us live in Texas than most people—even most Texans!—realize. Just give us some forested land, or at least a remote area with some cover, and some river bottom or a decent lake, and we get along just fine."

"The Sasquatch have been around in America for a long time. I read about a white man's report of a sighting that goes back to 1811. Indian legends about the Sasquatch go back for many centuries."

"We didn't just fall off the turnip truck," said Mr. Stomper.

I thought I could hear snickering, more like snorting, actually, from the surrounding darkness.

"Some people," I said, "believe you may have descended from Gigantopithecus, the largest of the primates, and migrated from Asia into the Americas over the ancient land bridge between Siberia and Alaska."

"That's an interesting concept," he said, totally noncommittal.

"Are you familiar with the fossilized dinosaur tracks in the limestone bed of the Paluxy River?" I asked.

"Near Glen Rose?"

"Some people claim that a Sasquatch made the smallest set of the tracks."

"That's absurd. Those tracks date back more than a hundred million years. The Sasquatch, just like Homo sapiens, don't go back that far. A small carnivorous dinosaur made the smaller tracks. It walked on its two back feet, which just happen to leave tracks about the size of Sasquatch tracks."

"I've read one account that says some Sasquatch males kidnapped some human women one time and married them."

"That's absurd. Human women are too homely."

"Have Sasquatch females ever kidnapped human men?"

"That's even more absurd. You men are even uglier. You have to face it. Your species lacks something when it comes to good looks." This time, I knew for certain that I could hear snorting from the surrounding darkness.

"From what I have read," I said, "most sightings of Sasquatch occur in the eastern half of the state, between the Abilene and Texarkana areas and from Red River down to the San Antonio and Huntsville areas."

"That's reasonable."

"Some places have tried to capitalize on the Sasquatch, or Bigfoot. At one time, a small town in the western part of Texas' Sasquatch range planned to have a Miss Bigfoot beauty pageant. The chamber of commerce thought that would attract a lot of tourists. Instead of a wet T-shirt contest, the citizens decided to have a wet sock contest. It turned into a big scandal.

They caught one of the girls padding her socks."

"Why would she wear socks?" asked Mr. Stomper, plainly puzzled. I could see him moving his bare feet, maybe even wiggling his toes, as if he had just taken off a pair of heavy boots after a long hike. I suddenly realized the source of the pungent Sasquatch smell, a new discovery I would have to report to the Bigfoot experts.

"A lot of Homo sapiens girls wear socks," I said, ready to move on with the interview. "I have read reports that the Sasquatch migrate, not along a north-south corridor, but along an east-west corridor."

"A few still do that," said Mr. Stomper.

"The people up around the little town of Direct, just south of Red River and about twenty miles northwest of Paris, say that they see the Sasquatch coming through in June headed west."

"A lot of us like to get out of that East Texas humidity during the summer."

"They see Sasquatch coming back through in October, headed east."

"The Sasquatch like to see the red oaks change color in the fall, after things cool off. Sometimes they go clear on over into Arkansas or Louisiana."

"People say they have seen Sasquatch out around Hawley and Haskell's Kiowa Peak, north of Abilene, and near Caddo, over by Breckenridge."

"That's about as far west as a Sasquatch can find decent cover."

"I've read reports of people seeing Sasquatch around Benbrook, Red Oak, and even Grand Prairie, right around Fort Worth and Dallas; Bosque County, southwest of Dallas/Fort Worth; near Denton; at Bells, out east of Sherman; Reno, just east of Paris; on Highway 31 east of Corsicana; Hallsville, Diana, and East Mountain, over around Longview; Lake Travis, out west of Austin; even Kelly Air Force Base in San Antonio. I feel sure that's just a sampling of the sightings."

"That all sounds reasonable," said Mr. Stomper.

"I've read about a sighting near Trinity, west of Athens," I said. "That's not far from where some workmen found the famous stone heads of Malakoff in a gravel pit back in 1929 . . . "

"The Sasquatch had nothing to do with those," Mr. Stomper interrupted.

"I thought perhaps I had solved a mystery."

"I wish we could help you. I've also wondered who carved those heads."

"There are some specific stories I want to ask you about. One happened at Lake Worth Nature Center back in 1969."

"That's the incident where one of our guys reportedly threw a tire five hundred feet? I have no comment on that story," said Mr. Stomper.

"Well, another story out of the Dallas/Fort Worth area: In May 1990 some young guys had camped at Lake Ray Roberts State Park, on the north side, and late in the night, they walked down through a stand of blackjack oak trees toward the water to go fishing. Something followed them. They got scared and ran back to their truck. They shone a small light at the trees. Something screeched and roared at them. They saw something moving through the trees. They got out of there.

"They came back the next night with a big spotlight and some guns. They heard the roar again. They put the spotlight on the trees and saw something that looked like a gigantic man. One of the boys fired at him with a shotgun. He roared even louder. He pushed over a middling-size cottonwood tree. The young guys took off and did not come back again until the following summer."

"I have no comment," said Mr. Stomper, "but I don't know why they would shoot at something that looked like a man."

I felt a little puzzled about his reluctance to confirm the stories. You would think that would be easy for him to do.

"A lot of people have seen Sasquatch around Texarkana," I said, "usually out in the longleaf pine forests close to the Arkansas border. Did the Sasquatch have anything to do with Arkansas' so-called 'Fouke Monster not far east of the Texas border'? Hollywood made a movie about it, *The Legend of Boggy Creek.*"

"Those might have been some of our boys out of the Arkansas, or maybe even the Louisiana, Division of Sasquatch," said Mr. Stomper. "Sometimes our ranges overlap."

I began to feel like I was interviewing a Washington politician. The fire had started to burn down now, casting Mr. Stomper even deeper into the shadows.

I said, "Back in 1975, a man from San Antonio went out to a private lake in an isolated area about thirty-five miles north of the city to fish. He heard a big—a BIG—splash in the water at the bottom of a sheer limestone cliff across a little neck of the lake, maybe two hundred yards away. He looked through a scope and saw a figure about eight or nine feet tall and covered with hair climbing up the cliff."

Mr. Stomper snorted. I realized by now that this was the Sasquatch laugh. It rumbled up from his belly. "Hughey Stomper," he said, snorting. "My nephew. That was Hughey Stomper. He went out to that lake to go fishing. That big old clumsy boy did love fishing. He fell off that cliff into the lake. His mama had told him not to go out there fishing. When he came home wet, she knew where he had been. She wore out his backside."

Finally, I had gotten Mr. Stomper to confirm a story! I thought that maybe now I might finally be getting someplace.

"On a hot night in the middle of the summer back in 1972, a family camping in Lake Somerville State Park heard a terrible scream. The darkness had really taken hold by then because the moon had set. Things had gotten still because the wind off the lake had died. The family dog ran and hid whimpering under the car. The family built a big campfire. One of the sons began firing a gun into the air. The family never saw a thing. The screams came again and again, eight more times that night. The next morning, the family could find nothing unusual around the camp except for a stand of saplings that had been snapped off about five or six feet above the ground."

"I have no comment on that story."

So he had reverted to "no comment." I began to feel frustrated. I had read a lot of other stories I wanted to confirm with Mr. Stomper, but by now, I had begun to doubt even his confirmation of the sighting at the lake north of San Antonio. I decided to skip over all of the remaining stories but one, but it would turn into a major scoop if I could only verify it. In fact, it would just about make my journalist career, maybe even make me rich, if Mr. Stomper could just confirm what I had read.

The fire had burned down considerably by now. No one moved to add wood.

"Mr. Stomper," I said, feeling almost as if I were speaking into empty darkness, "at least one researcher believes that there is a strong possibility of a connection between Unidentified Flying Objects—UFO's—and the Sasquatch. He offers a lot of circumstantial evidence. And he said that a Seattle, Washington, man, under hypnosis, recalled seeing two aliens descend from a hovering UFO and walk into a nearby wooded area near the city, followed by a Sasquatch. Can you authenticate a connection between UFO's and the Sasquatch?"

Mr. Stomper did not respond immediately. I believe that the question could have surprised him. I heard mumbling from the surrounding darkness. Finally Mr. Stomper said, "I have heard rumors that some of our intelligence agents have instructed aliens in the art of elusiveness. The principal rule is to never, never leave a verifiable clue of your existence. I emphasize that those are just rumors. You would have to go to our national officials to get corroboration."

Classic political evasiveness. The Texas Division Chief of the

Sasquatch would not give me a single really useful answer. Maybe this whole thing was a Bill Hada gag after all. I saw my future as a journalist dim. I lost patience. The campfire had burned down really low by now.

"Mr. Stomper," I asked, "why have you asked me out here for this interview? We are wasting time. I thought you wanted the true story of the Sasquatch to appear in print."

"The Sasquatch," Mr. Stomper said slowly, thoughtfully, "stand at a crossroads in our history."

It seemed that I could detect a new level of seriousness in his voice. "A crossroads? After all these centuries?"

"As a species, we have a major decision to make," he said. "You see, the Dallas Cowboys want to recruit Sasquatch to play on the team's offensive and defensive lines."

"The Dallas Cowboys?" I could not have been more stunned had a UFO fallen out of the sky.

"The Dallas Cowboys."

"How did they find you?"

"The Cowboys have an incredible scouting system."

"I find this hard to believe." This could turn into a more sensational story than a UFO connection.

"Think about it," said Mr. Stomper. "Our guys can stand nine feet tall and weigh a thousand pounds. They can rip up tree stumps. They can outrun a horse. They eat right. They are hard to pin down. They lead virtuous lives. If you don't count fishing.

"How would you like to play offensive tackle on an opposing team and have to block someone who stood two and a half feet taller than you, weighed seven hundred pounds more than you, could lift a Volkswagen, could run down your fastest guy like a greyhound on a rabbit, and could materialize and de-materialize at will?" asked Mr. Stomper.

"You'd have to have a lot of heart, give 110 percent on every play, and refine your blocking and tackling techniques," I said thoughtfully. "Why don't the Cowboys want you to play running back, or split end, or even quarterback? Those guys handle the ball and get all the glory."

"No opposing thumb," Mr. Stomper said. He thrust his enormous hand into the last flickering light of the fire for my inspection. "We're all fingers. That's worse than all thumbs when it comes to handling a football, but the scouts think we can learn to block and tackle."

I suddenly understood why the Sasquatch wanted the interview. They wanted a good, honest story about the species to be published coincident with their first appearance at Texas Stadium. They must not feel that they could trust the TV commentators. They could, of course, trust me. This could be the story of the decade. I could write a book and autograph copies at bookstores. Other journalists would write books about me.

"When are the Sasquatch going to report to the Cowboys' training camp?" I asked.

"We haven't made a decision yet. It would mean a major change in our traditional lifestyle."

"You would have to wear a helmet, a jersey, football pants, and pads."

"We know. We've discussed that."

"Of course, you would become rich and famous. The president might invite you to the White House when you won the Super Bowl. Television commentators would interview you before and after games. You could live in big houses in Northern California or the Texas Hill Country. You could play golf at the best country clubs. You could travel to eastern Asia, the Himalayan Mountains, and Europe and meet new relatives. You could go to London and see Big Ben and to Paris and see the Eiffel Tower."

"We've discussed those things, too."

"You'd have to wear shoes."

"Shoes?" I could hear a deep-throated grumbling rise out of the darkness beyond the trees as though there were a sense of alarm.

"Shoes. The National Football League rules say that each player has to wear a full uniform for protection. The only exception may be for punters and field goal specialists. Some of those guys like to kick with a bare foot. They don't get stepped on very often anyway."

"Shoes?" Mr. Stomper asked in disbelief.

"Shoes," I confirmed.

Suddenly, a terrible, agonizing scream cut through the darkness like a bowie knife, then another and another. Screams engulfed me like a tsunami of sound. I felt shell-shocked, immobilized. The screams died away slowly, making the night seem even darker than before. I realized the fire had gone completely out.

Mr. Stomper spoke from absolute blackness. He said, "I believe that the Texas Division of Sasquatch has just made a decision about whether we should play for the Dallas Cowboys."

"But what about the wealth and the fame and the travel?" I asked, seeing my story start to come apart.

"We'd have to wear shoes."

"What about the relatives and the big houses and the country clubs?"

"We'd have to wear shoes. Besides, we'd rather go fishing."

"What about my story on the Sasquatch?"
"Some other time."
"I just may write it in any event."
"That's all right. No one will believe you anyway."

Humming with the Hummers

ROCKPORT

The hummingbird, that lilliputian of the avian kingdom, touches the remoter corners of the human soul and tolls the bells of magic, spirituality, and ethereal beauty. Unique to the Western Hemisphere, it has left an enduring imprint on the American psyche.

For those with pre-Columbian roots, this glittering, gem like winged creature took up residence millennia ago in that mystical landscape usually reserved for the far grander eagle, hawk, raven, wild turkey, bear, cougar, wolf, coyote, deer, and mountain sheep. It has long played symbolic and often heroic roles in the arts and the crafts, the folklore and the mythology, the ritual and the ceremony of tribes, past and present, from the eastern woodlands of the Southeast to the deserts of the Southwest to the great plains of the central United States to the boreal woodlands of Canada and Alaska to the rain forests of Central America to the pampas of the Peruvian coast.

A shaman of an ancient hunting and foraging band chiseled a small figure of a hummingbird into the peak of a large boulder that rests on the floor of the Chihuahuan Desert in West Texas, not far from the community of Van Horn. Shamans carved other figures, abstract, unintelligible now, into the surfaces of the boulder's flanks surrounding the hummingbird. Anthropologists believe that shamans used such sites as gateways to the supernatural, or spirit, world, where they called on tribal deities to render abundance in nature, success in the hunt, healing from injury or illness, and relief from chronic tribal hardship. Presumably, the hummingbird served as an intermediary with the spirits.

I remember climbing to the top of the boulder some years ago along with my wife and several other people, including Richard S. "Scotty" MacNeish, an eminent archaeologist of the Americas, and we all wondered how something as delicate as a hummingbird could hold a spiritual place in the difficult lives of those early people.

One of the Apache tribes believed that the Creator made a hummingbird and dispatched it to survey His entire, newly formed earth and report the discoveries. Apaches believed, too, that a venerated young warrior named Wind Dancer returned as a hummingbird after he died while carrying out an errand of mercy. They knew that Wind Dancer, the warrior, and Wind Dancer, the hummingbird, were one and the same because both wore identical war paint.

The Mojaves, a tribe of Southern California, believed that the hummingbird delivered them to a new world when it discovered a passageway from their primeval subterranean chambers of perpetual darkness to the surface of the earth and the light of the sun.

Some of the puebo peoples of New Mexico and Arizona still paint hummingbirds on their water jars to celebrate its role in prevailing upon their deities to send rain for their crops.

The Hopis include a hummingbird kachina, Tocha Kachina, in their lexicon of masked dance figures, especially those of winter and spring.

The Chippewa, an Algonkian people of the western Great Lakes area, told of a young warrior named Odjibwa who changed himself into a hummingbird and then into a hummingbird's fluff to recover a magician's stolen scalp. The grateful magician gave a beautiful sister known as the Ruby Swan to Odjibwa for his wife.

Central America's Mayan people, founders of one of the Western Hemisphere's richest pre-Columbian cultures, believed that the sun masqueraded as an iridescent hummingbird, trying to win the heart of a beautiful young woman, the moon.

The Tarascan people, who occupied the Michoacan area west of today's Mexico City, built their capital on the shores of the exotic highland lake known as Patzcuaro. They called their city, with its pyramids and temples, Tzintzuntzan, a derivative of their word for "hummingbird," which they revered in their religion. Next to a stone and earthen temple platform a quarter of a mile long, the Tarascans constructed sunken pits in the shape of hummingbirds. They exported their hummingbirds' emerald plumage, symbolic of deities across southern and western Mexico, to neighboring peoples.

My wife and I visited Tzintzuntzan with two archaeologists, Tom O'Loughlin and his wife, Debbie Martin O'Loughlin, who had worked in Latin America, and a Mexican guide pointed out the hummingbird-shaped sunken pits, still clearly discernible after the passage of centuries.

To this day, the Tarascan women of Tzintzuntzan incorporate hummingbird designs into baskets they weave for their Dia de los Muertos, or

Day of the Dead, ceremonies, celebrated in early November each year to honor their ancestors. They are said to have learned basketry from a hummingbird, which taught them the craft in gratitude after a Tarascan woman gave it sugar water during a punishing drought.

The Aztec deity, Huitzilopochtli, which means "Southern Hummingbird," had tendrils if not roots in Tzintzuntzan, where the Aztec tribe once lived with the Tarascans. After they migrated eastward, the Aztecs adorned Huitzilopochtli's ritual headdress and costume with emerald hummingbird feathers, always from Michoacan.

As they built an empire crowned by the monumental architecture they raised at Mexico City, the Aztecs elevated Huitzilopochtli in the hierarchy of their gods, making him what one scholar called "their prime totemic symbol," their lord of creation. They constructed magnificent temples for worshiping Huitzilopochtli. They sacrificed hundreds of thousands of subjugated people to him, roasting them over a grill and ripping their hearts from their breasts, to satisfy the thirst of Huitzilopochtli, the Southern Hummingbird, for human blood. Aztec priests wrapped themselves in the bloody skins of victims and danced in celebration.

The pre-Columbian peoples of North and Central America cherished the hummingbird in their myth and ritual, scribing small figures into rocks and incorporating images on murals, ceramic vessels, or ritual dress. The Nascan peoples of Peru memorialized this sacred icon on a stunning scale, describing in stone outline a 164-foot-long figure of a hummingbird across the pampas near the coast of the Pacific Ocean. Created 1,500 to 2,500 years ago, the image is so large that it can be fully appreciated only from an aircraft.

The hummingbird moved pre-Columbian cultures of the Western Hemisphere spiritually, and they wove it into the fabric of myth and folklore. It moved the cultures of the Eastern Hemisphere materially when they arrived in the Americas, and the Europeans, especially, demanded the iridescent feathered hummingbird skins for collection and decoration. Traders in the Americas exported hundreds of thousands of hummingbird skins to London for sale through the city auction houses during the nineteenth century. French and Belgian craftsmen used the skins to make bonnets and fans.

The hummingbird's ability to beguile has persisted right into modern times.

In Mexico, today people wear stuffed hummingbirds as amulets and eat powdered hummingbird hearts to bring success in love.

In the United States, today people adopt the hummingbird as their totemic animal, i.e., an animal whose characteristics they admire and emulate. The "hummingbird people" try to participate in the hummingbird's world of ephemeral beauty, the entryway of crimson blooms, the taste of sweet nectars. They subscribe to its airy celebration of freedom and independence, its love of play and fun, its sense of fairy like enchantment. They seem to ignore or forget about the hummingbird's personality, which can be as contentious as a swarm of mad bees.

If the hummingbird interceded with the gods for ancient shamans, and if it enriches the lives of modern totemists, it astounds the ornithologist, who still has trouble comprehending this natural miracle.

• • •

At sunrise on a morning in the middle of March, a ruby-throated hummingbird, responding to some mysterious internal voice, rises from a forest or a field in Mexico—no one knows the exact location—and turns northward, over the landscape of the Maya, the Tarascans, the Aztecs, across the open waters of the Gulf of Mexico toward the coast of Texas.

With his bronze-green back and iridescent rubythroat reflecting the rays of the sun like polished metal, he has undertaken a difficult and solitary journey. No others of his kind accompany him.

Even though the rubythroat is an aerial acrobat—he can not only hover like a diminutive helicopter, he can fly backwards, side to side, or even, incredibly, upside down—he heads like an arrow toward Texas, possibly pointing toward a specific feeder he stored in his memories of the previous year—astonishingly, in a brain that weighs perhaps 1/100th of an ounce. He knows that if he is to complete a nonstop flight of some six hundred miles across the Gulf, he must budget his energy. He knows that he cannot rest in flight, for he lacks the ability to soar. He must fly continuously, relentlessly, until he reaches the distant opposite shore.

It seems impossible for so slight a creature, but the rubythroat comes from a clan of birds uniquely suited for the extraordinary. For its size, the hummingbird generates more energy than any other warm-blooded creature, and it possesses the largest heart of any warm-blooded creature and has the largest brain and the most elegantly developed skeletal structure and flight muscles of any bird. Even its organs are centered in its body to facilitate balanced flight. Altogether, 320 known species of hummingbirds are scattered across the Americas, most of them in the tropics.

The rubythroat, flying across the Gulf, would seem like a leaf in a hurricane.

His wingspan, tip to tip, measures no more than the width of a hand. His average weight, a tenth of an ounce, would not tip a small coin on a balance scale. His breathing rate exceeds four times a second. His heart throbs twenty times a second. His wings beat fifty times a second.

The rubythroat flies all day, all night, navigating, incomprehensibly, with a minuscule brain and no beacons, across the Gulf's waters at a rate of twenty-five miles per hour. During the passage, he beats his wings more than four million times. In an all but incomprehensible example of energy efficiency, he burns only 1/14th of an ounce of fat, the only baggage he packed for the trip, but that will equal 40 percent of what he weighed when he departed Mexico.

He arrives in Texas, near Rockport, at sunrise . . . hungry!

In fact, ravenous!!

Calling on his memory, he immediately checks the porch of a home where he had found a feeder with sugar water during his previous summer in Rockport. Failing there, he thankfully finds a trumpet creeper in early bloom. He dips his bill, like a thin straw, into blossom after blossom, greedily lapping nectar thirteen times a second with a long, split tongue.

He feeds on simple foods, which his digestive system can break down speedily and easily into nutrients and waste. The nutrients fuel his energy generation, which is prodigious: the hummingbird, relative to its weight, must consume more food than any other vertebrate on earth. (If we humans burned energy as rapidly as the hummingbird, we would have to consume twice our weight in meat every twenty-four hours.)

The rubythroat feeds, rests, and recovers from his marathon flight.

Other rubythroats, meanwhile, push on, headed for breeding grounds as far north as the Canadian provinces of Saskatchewan and Nova Scotia, more than 2,000 miles from their winter homes in Mexico.

Our rubythroat stakes out his territory, usually about half the size of a football field. Then he begins to behave absolutely boorishly, as if he thinks he is the big bird on the block.

He takes a high perch and announces his presence, shining like a rare jewel, but singing like a feathered Jimmy Durante.

After a bath in a pond or a rain shower, he dries and preens with all the vanity of a rock star, never knowing that he probably inherited his feathers, like all the other birds, from the homely dinosaurs. He uses his feet to groom the feathers of his head, neck, and throat, and his bill to groom the feathers of the rest of his body.

He laps at the sugar water of a feeder without gratitude, as though it were his due. Like a spoiled prince, he expects, almost demands, that the feeder be kept fresh and full. That is, after all, someone's job.

If another bird or an animal—of almost any species, including Homo sapiens—crowds his food source or interrupts his bath, our ill-tempered rubythroat may attack as if he believes he is Mike Tyson. If another hummingbird challenges him, he may use his bill like a rapier, trying to pierce his opponent's eyes.

Little wonder that hummingbirds lead solitary lives.

Let a lady hummingbird, even one of another species, give the slightest hummingbird wink to our rubythroat, however, and his entire personality changes. At least for the moment.

He makes a damn fool of himself.

He flutters his feathers to demonstrate their sheen, and he sings (probably a mistake) as if he thinks he is Roy Rogers serenading Dale Evans. Let the lady hummingbird show the least interest, and our rubythroat goes into an ecstasy of flight, climbing, diving, swooping through arc after arc, always mindful of how the sun's rays illuminate the iridescence of his bronze-green and red colors. He behaves as though he thinks he is a stunt pilot, complete with helmet, goggles, and flowing white scarf, in an open-cockpit Steerman.

If she submits in spite of his showboating (or, conceivably, I guess, because of it), the marriage is probably one of the shortest on record: three to five seconds. The time it takes for consummation. No more.

His conquest complete, our rubythroat immediately abandons his new bride. He returns to feeding, bathing, preening, fighting, chasing other lady hummingbirds, and generally having a good time.

Knowing ahead of time what she was getting herself into, the lady hummingbird had already constructed and even decorated her nest, a tiny cup about the diameter of a nickel, and she has lined it carefully and lovingly with down or spiderweb. She will now lay two eggs about the size of kernels of corn and will raise her family alone, probably glad to be rid of that fellow with the gaudy red throat.

At sunrise on a morning in the middle of October, our rubythroat, responding to some mysterious internal voice, rises from the Gulf coast at Rockport and turns southward, over the open waters of the Gulf of Mexico; across the coast of Mexico, above the landscape of the Aztecs, the Tarascans, and the Maya, to his secret winter retreat. With his bronze-green back and iridescent ruby throat reflecting the rays of the sun like polished metal, he has undertaken a difficult and solitary journey. No others of his kind accompany him.

With luck, he will probably return to Rockport next March and maybe for another season or two, reminding us of the magic he has spun, enchanting us with his unerring sense of beauty and his sense of irascible selfishness and fun.

The brilliantly colored little scoundrel has gotten inside the heads of numerous poets, flying, for example, right out of the lyric words of Emily Dickinson.

> *He never stops, but slackens*
> *Above the Ripest Rose—*
> *Partakes without alighting*
> *And praises as he goes.*

It's hard to believe that the hummingbird descended from dinosaurs.

Postscript

The rubythroat, one of eighteen species that visit Texas during the summer, ranges across the eastern two thirds of the state. Many rubythroats congregate at Rockport in the fall, fattening up for their return to their winter homes. Rockport celebrates their stay in September of each year.

That Night at The Vaudeville

VAUDEVILLE THEATER

King Fisher, a killer, an outlaw, a cattle baron, an ex-convict, and a lawman, came to town. He met up with Ben Thompson, a killer, a gambler, a soldier, an ex-convict, and a lawman, whom Fisher did not even respect, let alone like, and they got drunk together in the saloons around Congress Avenue, in downtown Austin.

Fisher said, "Thompson, let's get on the train and go down to San Antonio," and Thompson said he did not want to get on the train with Fisher and go down to San Antonio," but they did. Once there, Fisher said, "Thompson, let's go over to the Vaudeville Theater," and Thompson said he did not want to go over to the Vaudeville with Fisher, but they did.

No one will ever know why Fisher, who could have expected nothing short of calamity, insisted that Thompson go to San Antonio and the Vaudeville with him. No one can ever fully explain the chaotic violence that erupted that night at the Vaudeville. It is an abiding mystery.

It all happened on Tuesday, March 11, 1884.

Alone, armed, drinking hard, either Fisher or Thompson evoked a sense of danger, like a menacing tiger shark, its fin slicing the water's surface.

Together . . . together, armed, drinking hard, they reached into the darkest corners of human fear and scattered men as if they were a startled school of fish.

And with good reason.

King Fisher once said that he had killed seven men, and "I don't count Mexicans."

By his early twenties, during the mid-1870's, King Fisher ruled like a feudal baron over a southwestern Texas border area that was larger than the state of Massachusetts. From the headquarters of his ranch on the Pendencia River, near Carrizo Springs in Dimmit County, he ran a gang of more than a hundred outlaws. He and his followers rustled cattle and horses and shot men on both sides of the Rio Grande. He controlled the courts and the crime. He posted a sign at the gate where his ranch road intersected a main wagon road: "This is King Fisher's road," it said. "Take the other."

Mrs. Albert Maverick, Sr., spoke of a fearful night which King Fisher spent at her home in Bandera County: "After all was quiet, I spent a very restless time—and one time when he got up to get a drink of water from the bucket, I held my baby very tight thinking we would die together," she said. "I didn't realize he was a man-killer, not a baby-killer."

A killer, a tyrant. But King Fisher had charisma, charm, which made him even more dangerous. Powerful men protected him. Ruthless thugs followed him. Beautiful women pursued him. Many people *liked* King Fisher. They told as many tales of his kindnesses as they did of his killings.

Six feet tall, muscular, and twenty-eight years old that March of 1884, he had a dark complexion, dark hair, intent eyes (one black, one brown), and a heavy mustache. He often wore a Mexican sombrero and a buckskin jacket, both decorated with gold. He wore a pair of silver-plated, ivory-handled revolvers at his sides. Moving with the grace of an Olympic gymnast, he could kill you with either hand.

He killed three Mexican men who tried to recover a stolen horse from his corrals, three more who tried to recover stolen cattle (plus a few of Fisher's own stock) from his pastures, and four more who disputed their unexpectedly small share of rustled cows.

By sixteen, King Fisher had served four months at the Huntsville State Penitentiary for burglarizing a home in Goliad. He grew as hard as an anvil, forged by a term in the pen.

When the Texas Rangers, under famed Captain Lee Hall, caught up with King Fisher at his Pendencia ranch, he found himself charged with five counts of murder, a count of assault with intent to murder, and counts of cattle rustling and horse theft. And those were just the crimes in Texas.

At twenty-five, Fisher spent nine months in the San Antonio jail known as Bat Cave, where the winged mammals had taken up residence in the second story. The stern-looking jail, a half block north of the Governor's Palace and Military Plaza, was surrounded by a high wall topped with glass from broken bottles.

Friends did not forget King Fisher in Bat Cave. His close friend Joe Foster, a bespectacled, small, frail, and scarred Civil War veteran, sent him meals from the outside, never charging him a cent for the favor. Joe Foster and two other close San Antonio friends, Jack "Pegleg" Harris and Billy Simms, owned the Vaudeville Theater, where Fisher and Thompson would go that fateful March night.

Released from Bat Cave in 1879, King Fisher spent two more years digging his way out from under his legal troubles, with the weight of possible imprisonment finally lifting after a series of acquittals and case dismissals.

And King Fisher reformed.

He grew no less dangerous. He just reformed.

He moved to the other side of the law enforcer's badge and became the chief deputy sheriff of Uvalde County, serving under Sheriff Ben Boatright.

Fisher's skill with a gun now became an asset rather than a threat to a community. He made his mark in law enforcement as rapidly as he had risen to cattle baron. He soon took on Uvalde's notorious Hannehan family, including the mother, Mary, and her three sons, Tom, Jim, and John. The Hannehans had been indicted for numerous crimes, including murder and cattle rustling.

Tom and Jim made the mistake of robbing the San Antonio–to–El Paso stage while Fisher served as deputy sheriff. He tracked them to their ranch. They resisted arrest. Fisher shot Tom to death, arrested Jim, and recovered their plunder.

King Fisher was still dangerous.

Mary Hannehan never forgave Fisher. She would never forget.

She would never forget.

Dawn, one day in 1860. Ben Thompson stood in the dim morning light, next to a vacant icehouse in New Orleans, his fist locked around the handle of his bowie knife, staring hard at the Frenchman Emile de Tours.

De Tours, his fist gripping the handle of his own bowie knife, stared grimly back at Thompson.

If de Tours searched for fear in the eyes of this eighteen-year-old boy he now meant to kill, he probably found instead a cold and unnerving intensity, like that in the eyes of a timber wolf stalking its prey.

De Tours may have had second thoughts then about challenging young Thompson to a duel, but it was too late. There was no choice. It was a question of honor.

Thompson had insulted the Frenchman some weeks earlier when he put a stop to de Tours' groping attack on a young woman in a horse-drawn omnibus in the downtown streets of New Orleans. He jerked the Frenchman away from the woman, fought with him, stabbed him in the shoulder, and threw him from the vehicle. Thompson would have killed de Tours then, but the Frenchman's friends intervened.

When de Tours healed, he challenged Thompson to the duel.

According to the code of dueling, Thompson had the choice of conditions and weapons. He elected to fight in the icehouse, its door closed, its interior as black as death. He selected bowie knives, which had heavy, thick blades, perhaps ten inches in length, as weapons. De Tours recoiled at Thompson's barbarous proposal, but he could not reject it. It was a question of honor.

Ben Thompson and Emile de Tours stepped inside and heard the heavy thud of the icehouse door as their seconds slammed it shut and locked it from the outside. It shut out any light as completely as a closed lid seals light from a casket. There was no escape. They must search through the tomblike blackness until they found one another and fight without ever seeing each other until one of them died.

"Are you ready?" asked Thompson, immediately stepping silently away from his position.

De Tours did not answer. He lunged through the blackness and stabbed at the sound of Thompson's voice. De Tours had telegraphed his location.

As unerring as a rattlesnake striking a rat in the inky tunnel of its nest, Thompson found the Frenchman and drove the broad blade of the bowie knife into his body. Thompson felt de Tours slump to the floor. He made sure de Tours was finished. He then groped his way through the blackness to the door. He rapped. The heavy door swung open. Dim light penetrated into the gloom, illuminating de Tours's lifeless body.

Thompson fled New Orleans, the city police, and de Tours' vengeful friends. He rode westward to Austin, the town where he had lived during his early teens.

Thompson, who had already shot and wounded at least three people, battled Comanches, and killed at least one Indian before he killed de Tours, had set a life course measured in terms of violence and death. It was almost as if he was addicted to the visceral thrill of gunfire and killing.

He took up gambling as a profession. He killed men in disputes over cards. He joined the Confederate army and fought against Union forces at the Gulf coast. He joined the Mexican emperor Maximilian's forces and fought against rebels south of the border. He served time in the Austin county jails, San Antonio's Bat Cave, and Huntsville's state penitentiary—all hellholes of existence. He operated gambling halls in cattle trail towns from Texas to Kansas and in railroad towns in Colorado. He attracted violence like a lightning rod attracts lightning.

He described his killing of a man at a fandango, or dance, somewhere in Mexico: "He . . . had his hand on his knife. He seemed to hesitate a moment, but only a moment, drew quickly and dashed at me. I was just in time; a step sideways and backward avoided the blow. I struck him on the head with my pistol, and then, as rapidly as thought, shot him four times. I don't think he even moved after he fell—and he commenced falling on the first shot—nor did I shoot after he touched the floor."

If Thompson, a man about five feet nine inches tall with black hair and blue eyes, triggered fear through his violence and killings, he evoked respect and even affection for his kindnesses. He rescued an immigrant boy from the abuses of a brutal boss. He contributed to charitable organizations. He arranged and paid for the care of orphan children in Austin.

He ran for and won the election for city marshal of Austin in 1880, and he put a stop to violent crime. Not one murder, assault with intent to murder, or burglary occurred during Thompson's watch.

Then one day in July of 1882, he took the train down to San Antonio, and he went over to the Vaudeville Theater. Like a reformed boozer falling off the wagon, Thompson soon yielded to the old craving for violence and killing. He argued with King Fisher's close friends, Vaudeville owners Jack Harris, Joe Foster, and Billy Simms. He goaded Harris, a Civil War veteran with a crippled left hand, into a confrontation and shot him to death.

Thompson surrendered the next morning to Sheriff McCall and Marshall Shardein, who threw him into the Bat Cave. He spent six months in that squalid jail. He resigned as Austin's city marshal. Although a San Antonio jury acquitted him and he returned home to Austin and a hero's welcome, he sank into despair as if it were quicksand.

His world had come unraveled. Not only had he given up his job as city marshal, but he learned that he had just lost an old and trusted friend in New Orleans. His mother lay on her deathbed. His brother, Billy, wild and given to violence in his own right, languished in jail for a crime committed in Refugio County years before. His gambling business had eroded. And he had made deep and enduring enemies of the surviving Vaudeville partners, Joe Foster and Billy Simms.

Thompson reached for his old and trusted emotional lifeline, alcohol, and sometimes at night, suffering from insomnia, he shot up the town just for the hell of it.

That was the condition in which King Fisher found Ben Thompson in Austin that Tuesday, March 11, 1884. We shall never know what drew the two together. They had argued in the past. Fisher had said he felt nothing but contempt for Thompson. He lost his good friend Jack Harris to Thompson's pistol. He still maintained close friendships with Foster and Simms, perhaps Thompson's worst enemies. Fisher seldom drank.

It seemed like an implausible union, but on the surface, at least, alcohol on that day appeared to convert two old adversaries into two new friends, an alliance that reeked of danger. Men watched the pair warily, like buffalo watched wolves stalking a herd.

Fisher and Thompson had plenty of places in Austin to find a drink.

The city, home to the state capitol, a brand-new university, and about eleven thousand residents, had emerged as what one citizen called "a gay place, filled with cowmen, flush of money, rearing to spend it on gambling, booze, and the women of the night." Its population surged with the arrival of the railroad in 1871, and Austin had eighty saloons by the 1880's, some twenty gambling halls, and several famed bawdy houses. They clustered near Congress Avenue, with its new brick buildings, gaslights, horse-drawn cars, and still-unpaved street.

On the surface, at least, Fisher and Thompson had a good time there, but Fisher wanted to go to San Antonio. He began insisting that Thompson take the train and go with him. Thompson resisted, haunted by visions of his enmity with Foster and Simms. He especially wanted to avoid the Vaudeville. "I know if I were to go into that place," he had said earlier, "it would be my graveyard."

Joe Foster, Fisher's good friend from his days in Bat Cave, had declared that Ben Thompson could never enter the Vaudeville Theater again.

Still, Fisher insisted that they go to San Antonio together. Alcohol does strange things to a man's mind and to his common sense, so Thompson finally agreed.

They got to the railroad station late, as the train pulled away from the

Austin depot. They commandeered a carriage, caught up with the train where it slowed for its Colorado River crossing, and jumped from the moving carriage to the moving cars.

Like a weather forecaster tracking a killer storm, someone—who would not reveal his name—telegraphed Joe Foster and Billy Simms at the Vaudeville that Fisher and Thompson, armed and drinking hard, now bore down on San Antonio. Simms, a clean-shaven, twenty-eight-year-old man with a thick shock of hair combed to the right side of his head, rushed over with the telegram to show it to Marshal Shardein. The marshal said that according to the law, nothing could be done until trouble started. His police, however, instructed people who might come into contact with Thompson to kill the man if he gave them the slightest excuse. That might be easier said than done.

Simms next showed the telegram to a local judge. Buy a shotgun, advised the judge. Simms bought a shotgun.

Foster and Simms, uncertain of the support offered by Shardein, took precautions of their own. They instructed their own special officer, or club bouncer, Jacob S. Coy, to shadow Fisher and Thompson if the two appeared at the Vaudeville.

And they hired three assassins: a bartender named McLaughlin, a gambler known as Canada Bill and a variety performer called Harry Tremaine. They paid the assassins two hundred dollars. They would secrete them in a Vaudeville theater box, armed with Winchester rifles.

Meanwhile, Fisher and Thompson had a raucous time on the train to San Antonio. They took a bottle of whiskey away from a German passenger and drained it. Thompson smashed the bottle over the head of a black porter for some trivial offense and drew a tough rebuke from Fisher. Thompson cut away the crown of his beaver hat, stained by the porter's blood, and wore the brim, apparently as a joke, into San Antonio when they arrived at eight o'clock that night.

The heart of San Antonio, two and a half times larger than Austin, beat to the rhythms of its Spanish and Mexican origins. Spanish-style plazas, a cauldron of activity day and night, served as open-air markets. Vendors sold their produce from the backs of wagons. Chili vendors at open stands sold foods that contained, according to *Scribners* magazine, "various savory compounds, swimming in fiery pepper, which biteth like a serpent." Bullfighting had ended only a few years earlier. Fandangos and cockfighting continued.

While Austin's growth slowed in the 1880's, San Antonio exploded. Rail service, a telephone exchange, electric streetlights, and breweries had made their appearance. A grand opera house, a new post office and federal building, a new hospital, and many new businesses would soon open. As in Austin, gambling halls, saloons and a red-light district flourished.

Fisher and Thompson went directly from the train station for drinks at Gallagher's Saloon, where Thompson explained to presumably amused patrons what had happened to his hat.

Meanwhile, Joe Foster, Billy Simms, and Jacob Coy waited anxiously to see whether Fisher and Thompson would come to the Vaudeville.

The two went from Gallagher's Saloon to the Turner Hall Opera House, at the intersection of Houston and St. Mary's Streets, three blocks west of the Alamo, to see a celebrated actress, Ada Gray, play the leading role in a production called *East Lynne*.

Seated in the front of the theater, on the left side, with guns at their sides and Thompson still wearing his mutilated hat, the pair created a stir in the audience. People knew these were two of the most notorious gunmen in Texas.

Foster, Simms, and Coy waited at the Vaudeville, their anxiety growing.

Fisher and Thompson drank in the opera house bar between acts. They left Turner Hall just before the final curtain. It was now about 10:30 p.m., March 11, 1884.

Fisher said, "Let's go to the Vaudeville." Thompson said no. Fisher would not accept no, even though he knew the potential for trouble and a friend warned the two men not to go there. Fisher insisted—demanded—that they go to the Vaudeville. Finally, Thompson relented. They took a hack for a two-or three-block ride to where Foster, Simms, and Coy waited.

The Vaudeville, perhaps the most famous bar, variety-show theater and gambling hall in San Antonio, stood near the northwest corner of the intersection of Commerce and Soledad Streets, near the main plaza, the heart of the city. A sign above the entrance said:

> Open Every Night
> VAUDVILLE
> THEATRE

The bar and variety-show theater occupied the second building west from the corner. The gambling hall occupied the second floor of the building on the corner. Sim Hart's tobacco shop occupied the first floor of the corner building. Advertising signs for Hart's shop covered the south and east outside walls of the corner building. A bizarre rendering of a man's face, laughing maniacally, as if in mockery of the onrushing drama, dominated the east wall.

Fisher and Thompson stopped first for a drink in the Vaudeville bar, the very room in which Thompson had shot Jack Harris to death twenty months earlier.

Billy Simms, unarmed, came into the bar. He had left the shotgun he had bought for the occasion on the stairs in the theater.

"Hello, Ben," said Simms. "I'm glad to see you." As ordered, Jacob Coy quickly joined the group. Everyone shook hands.

"Ben, I'm awful glad to see you here," said Simms. "Let's forget the past and be friends in the future."

"I desire to be friends," said Thompson, "and I have come here with my friend Fisher to talk the matter over and have a perfect understanding. I have a perfect right to do that, have I not?"

"Yes, Ben, that is right and I know we can be friends."

"I have nothing against you or Foster," said Thompson. "I am not afraid of you. I . . . want to be friends with you and I have come to talk it over."

By this time, the three assassins had taken their station in the theater box overlooking the balcony.

"That's all right," Simms said. "Come upstairs and see Foster."

Fisher and Thompson went upstairs to the theater balcony. Simms and Coy delayed following them. A girl, in a short skirt and red stockings, one of several who worked for a percentage of sales, came by to take their drink orders. Foster did not appear. Thompson grew uneasy.

Unknown to Fisher and Thompson, Coy had alerted a constable named Casanovas and two assistant marshals that the two gunmen had moved to the balcony.

Coy then came to the balcony and took a seat to the right of Fisher. Simms joined them, sitting to the left of Thompson.

The girl delivered their drink orders. Thompson teased her, saying that he could not pay, then he pulled out a large roll of bills and paid her.

He turned to Simms and said, "I thought you brought me up here to see Foster." He turned threatening. "Billy, don't play any games on me."

"It's just as I told you, Ben," said Simms. "I will go and tell Foster you want to have a friendly talk with him."

"Yes, go and get him," said Fisher. "I want to make you fellows good friends before I leave. Thompson is willing to do so and I want Foster to come over and meet him halfway." No one knows whether Fisher had any suspicion that his old friends Foster and Simms had law enforcement officers standing at alert and hired assassins now crouched in ambush.

"All right," said Simms. "I will go and get him."

Momentarily, Simms returned with Foster, adjusting his eyeglasses with his thin hands as he arrived.

Thompson extended his hand, but got no response. The tension suddenly rose.

Sensing the danger, Fisher tried to defuse the situation. He said to Foster, the man who had nurtured him in his Bat Cave days, "I want you and Thompson to be friends. I want you to shake hands like gentlemen."

"I cannot shake hands with Ben Thompson," said Foster, standing well clear, "nor can he and I be friends, and I want him to keep out of my way."

Ben Thompson, his anger welling up, his voice rising, asked Foster in disbelief if he refused to shake hands. Simms and Coy asked Thompson to keep his voice down so he would not disturb the audience in the theater.

"I can't shake hands with you," said Foster, standing well clear of Thompson, "and all I ask, Ben, is to be let alone, and I told Billy to tell you I never would put a straw in your way. The world is wide enough for both of us."

All at once, Simms and Coy stepped clear from Fisher and Thompson, whose old killer instincts suddenly kicked in through the haze of a long day of drinking. The two gunfighters came to their feet and tried to get their backs to the wall. Rifle fire erupted from above them, cutting down Simms' and Foster's supposed friend King Fisher and their certain enemy Ben Thompson.

Frenzied, as if fearing that Fisher and Thompson might rise from the dead to take retribution, Simms and Coy snatched the gunfighters' revolvers from the holsters and poured shot after shot into the dead men's heads and bodies. Foster tried to draw his own revolver and shot himself in the leg. A stray shot struck Coy in the leg.

The Vaudeville Theater exploded into pandemonium. Women screamed. Patrons crashed through windows onto Commerce Street to escape. Performers bolted the stage. The piano player dove for cover. Glass shattered. Tables and chairs overturned, smashing to the floor.

Marshal Shardein, poised in front of the Vaudeville in anticipation of trouble, heard the shots and raced through the building and up the stairs to the balcony. He passed Foster, as frantic men carried him, bleeding profusely, down the steps to get help.

Someone yelled that Ben's brother, Billy, by coincidence in San Antonio at a saloon a few doors away, had already heard the news and was headed toward the Vaudeville in a rage and armed with a shotgun. Shardein ran back down the steps, now covered with Foster's blood, to head off Billy, who arrived emotionally devastated and unarmed.

The gunfire over, people surged up the stairs and onto the balcony to get a firsthand look at the bodies of King Fisher and Ben Thompson. Women dragged the hems of their long skirts through the pools of blood to see for themselves the mangled corpses of the famed gunfighters. "Which is Ben?" they asked. "Show me Ben. Is that him?"

The two men lay side by side, Fisher's arm lying across Thompson as if to protect him. Crimson blood coated their faces and hair. Fisher, after a lifetime of violence and killing, looked somehow peaceful and serene. Ben Thompson's blue eyes looked into the nothingness of death.

The following morning, Carter and Mullaly, local undertakers, moved the bodies from the Vaudeville to police facilities at Bat Cave, where both of the gunfighters had served their time. Examiners counted thirteen wounds from rifle and revolver fire in Fisher's body, nine in Thompson's body.

Assassins McLaughlin, Canada Bill, and Harry Tremaine had done their jobs well. In the confusion, they escaped the Vaudeville undetected and soon fled the country and the pages of history.

The next day, March 12, 1884, Justice Anton Adam convened a

six-man coroner's jury, which viewed the bodies and heard testimony. The jury retired and, within ten minutes, returned its verdict: "The said killing was justifiable and done in self-defense in the immediate danger of life." No one would be charged with murder. The jury ignored the evidence for assassination.

Controversy arose immediately.

Why was King Fisher so insistent that Ben Thompson accompany him to the Vaudeville, where he knew that almost inevitably there would be trouble?

Did he set Thompson up for murder?

Did Billy Simms and Joe Foster, supposed friends, betray Fisher and order him killed, too?

Or did the assassins simply capitalize on an opportunity to murder two famed gunmen?

It is a controversy that will never be resolved, never be explained. Historians debate the issues to this day. The answer is buried with the men who fired the rifles and revolvers in the balcony and from the theater box that bloody night at the Vaudeville.

Deputy U.S. Marshal Ferd Niggli, a good friend, came to San Antonio to take King Fisher's body home by train to Uvalde, where the entire city turned out to join his wife and three daughters in mourning. His body lies buried today under the spreading arms of a great live oak tree at the Pioneer Cemetery, on Old Town Street.

Billy Thompson claimed Ben's body and took it home to Austin. After the funeral, on March 13, the Knights of Pythias, leading a cortege of sixty-two vehicles, conducted the coffin to Oakwood Cemetery for burial. Orphans whom Thompson had helped during his lifetime wept at his graveside.

Several days later, Joe Foster died in San Antonio, a victim of a self-inflicted wound, ironically, in the same house and room where Jack Harris had died twenty months earlier, the last man killed by Thompson.

Jacob Coy became a cripple as a result of the wound he received during the shooting.

Billy Simms somehow escaped injury from the hail of gunfire. He assisted Coy financially for the remainder of the policeman's life. In his later years, Simms emerged as a civic leader in San Antonio. He became president of the San Antonio International Fair Association.

Finally, Uvalde's notorious Mary Hannehan would not let go of her grudge against King Fisher even in his death. For years, she came to King Fisher's grave on the anniversary of his killing of her son Tom. She built a fire of brush at his headstone and danced like a demon around the flames.

Postscript
Bat Cave was replaced by a six-story structure early in the twentieth century. Most of the wall structure that once surrounded the jail, however, remains in place, a convenient support for utility meter and switch boxes. The Turner Hall Opera House and the Vaudeville Theater have long since been replaced by multistory buildings. Not a single historic marker speaks to those dramatic events that played out that Tuesday night, March 11, 1884.

MAJOR SOURCES

HOW DO I KNOW A GHOST IF I SEE ONE?
Boatright, M. C., W. M. Hudson, and A. Maxwell. *Texas Folk and Folklore*. Dallas: Southern Methodist University Press, 1954.
Galveston Historical Foundation. Web Site, Internet.
Scoville, J. Ghost City Texas. Texas Monthly Web Site, Internet.
Williams, D. S. *Ghosts Along the Texas Coast*. Plano, Tex.: Wordware Publishing, 1955.

RESURRECTION OF BUCK CREEK
Bennett, C. T. *Our Roots Grow Deep: A History of Cottle County*. Floydada, Texas: Blanco Offset Printing, 1970.
Woodley, M. Personal communication, mid-1950s.

KONATE'S STAFF
Brown, Jr., W. R. "Comancheria Demography, 1805–1830." *Panhandle-Plains Historical Review*, 59 (1986): 1–17.
Capps, Benjamin. *The Great Chiefs*. Old West Series. Alexandria, Va: Time-Life Books, 1975.
Grimes, J. "Piece of Kiowa Past Found in Park." *Lawton Constitution*, November 11, 1997.
Marriott, A. *Saynday's People: The Kiowa Indians and the Stories They Told*, Lincoln: University of Nebraska Press, 1963.
The Ten Grandmothers: Epic of the Kiowas. Norman: University of Oklahoma Press, 1989.
Mayhall, M. P. *The Kiowas*. Norman: University of Oklahoma Press, 1989.
Momaday, N. S. *The Way to Rainy Mountain*. Albuquerque: University of New Mexico Press, 1960.
Mooney, J. "Calendar History of the Kiowa Indians." *Seventeenth Annual Report of the Bureau of American Ethnology to the Secretary of the Smithsonian Institution, 1895–96*.
Noyes, S. *Los Comanches: The Horse People, 1751–1845*. Albuquerque: University of New Mexico Press, 1993.
Nye, W. S. *Bad Medicine and Good Tales of the Kiowas*. Norman: University of Oklahoma Press, 1962.
Tsonetokoy, D., Sr. Personal communication, 1997.

True Believer
Block, J., and D. Byrd. Ball Lightning and Earthquake Lights. Earth and Sky Online, Web Site, Internet.

Chariton, W. O., C. Eckhardt, and K. R. Young. *Unsolved Texas Mysteries.* Plano, Tex.: Wordware Publishing, 1990.

Krystek, L. Mirages in the Sky. Krystek Web Site, Internet.

Miles, E. *Tales of the Big Bend.* College Station: Texas A&M University Press, 1976.

Neider, C. *The Autobiography of Mark Twain.* New York. Harper and Row, 1959.

Plimpton, G. Interview with Ernest Hemingway. "The Art of Fiction." *Paris Review* (Spring 1958): 60–89.

Rees, R. R. The James Dean Mystery Ghost Lights of Marfa, Texas. Robert Rees Web Site, Internet.

The Stone Heads of Malakoff
Dixon, E. J. *Quest for the Origins of the First Americans.* Albuquerque: University of New Mexico Press, 1993.

Environmental Protection Agency. The Ice Age, Gulf of Mexico Program. Web Site, Internet.

Forbis, R. G. *The Paleoamericans: North America.* St. Martin's Series in Prehistory. New York: St. Martin's Press, 1975.

Kurten, B., and E. Anderson. *Pleistocene Mammals of North America.* New York: Columbia University Press, 1980.

Newcomb, W. W., Jr. *The Indians of Texas.* Austin: University of Texas Press, 1965.

Sellards, E. H. *Early Man in America.* Austin: Texas Memorial Museum. "Stone Images from Henderson County, Texas." *American Antiquity* (July–April): 1941/1942: 29–38.

Southern Methodist University Anthropology Department. Prehistoric Artifacts and Settlement Patterns in Dallas, Native American Presence in Area. Web Site, Internet.

Welch, J. R. *People and Places in the Texas Past.* Dallas: G.L.A. Press, 1974.

Interview with Cheetwah
"America Baffles Gold Hunters." *El Paso Times*, January 8, 1922.

"Canyon Trip Well Worth Fee." *El Paso Herald Post*, July 30, 1939.

Dobie, J. Frank. *Coronado's Children.* Austin: University of Texas Press, 1988.

"El Pasoans Seek Mine Near Here Abandoned by Franciscan Fathers." *El Paso Herald Post*, June 13, 1930.

"5800-Foot Mountain Picnic Park Only 14 Miles from Downtown El Paso." *El Paso Herald Post*, July 3, 1937.

"Has Ghost Fire of Lost Padre Mine Returned to the Franklin Mountains?" *El Paso Herald Post*, November 2, 1973.

"Indian Spring Near El Paso Flowing Water." *El Paso Times*, July 10, 1938.

Kottlowski, B. L. "The Lost Padre Mine." *New Mexico Magazine* (October 1966): 22–36.

Lane, E. C. "The Legend of Cheetwah." In *J. Frank Dobie Legends of Texas.* Vol. 2, *Pirates' Gold and Other Tales.* Gretna, La.: Pelican Publishing, 1995.

"Legend Dates to 1650." *El Paso Herald Post*, May 7, 1972.

"Magazine Article Features El Pasoan Who Knows of Lost Mine." *El Paso Herald Post*, April 19, 1971.

Meanley, T. "Lost Mine Ghost Fire Is Dancing Again in Indian Springs Canyon Near El Paso." *El Paso Herald Post*, April 21, 1939.

Parish, J. "Does Mount Franklin Hide Riches?" Unsourced newspaper clipping, July 30, 1950, El Paso Public Library.

"Prospector Believes Treasure May Be Buried in Franklins." *El Paso Times*, April 28, 1951.

"(....) Still Lures Prospectors." *El Paso Herald Post*, January 16, 1961.

Stevens, W. B. (special correspondent of the *St. Louis Globe Democrat*). "The Lost Mine and the Ancient Church on the Rio Grande: A Series of Interesting Letters." September 3, 1892. El Paso Public Library.

Texas Parks and Wildlife. Park and Historic Sites. Web Site, Internet.

Villalobos, R. "Search for Lost Padre Mine." *El Paso Times*, April 28, 1974.

"Legends of Gold Surround Franklins as Well as Victorio." *El Paso Times*, March 25, 1977.

THE MYSTERY OF THE LADY IN BLUE

The Blue Nun, The Mysterious Valley Home Page. Web Site, Internet.

Bolton, H. E. "The Spanish Occupation of Texas." *Southwestern Historical Quarterly* (July 1912): 1–26.

Evans, E. H. "The Mysterious Lady in Blue." *Arizona Highways* (September 1959): 1–26.

Fehrenbach, T. R. *Lone Star: A History of Texas and the Texans.* New York: Macmillan Publishing Company, Collier Books, 1980.

Hodge, F. W., G. P. Hammond, and A. Rey. *Fray Alonso de Benavides, Revised Memorial of 1634.* Albuquerque: University of New Mexico Press, 1945.

Karney, B. Mary Agreda. "The Lady in Blue." A Study of Mary of Agreda, Spain—Seventeenth-Century Franciscan Abbess. Web Site, Internet.

Kenney, M. M. "Tribal Society Among Texas Indians." *Quarterly of the Texas State Historical Association-* 1 (July 1897–April 1898): 26–33.

McCaleb. *Spanish Missions of Texas.* San Antonio: Naylor, 1961.

Miller, R. R. *Mexico: A History.* Norman: University of Oklahoma Press, 1985.

Schmitt, E. J. P. "Ven. María Jesús de Agreda: A Correction." *Quarterly of the Texas State Historical Association-* 1 (July, 1897–April 1898): 121–24.

Shea, J. G. *History of the Catholic Missions Among the Indian Tribes of the United States. 1529–1854.* New York: AMS Press, 1973.

Williams, M. *The Story of Spain.* Malaga, Spain: Ediciones Santana, S.L., 1996.

Yoakum, Esq., H. *History of Texas From Its First Settlement in 1685 to its Annexation to the United States in 1846.* Facsimile reproduction. Austin: Steck Company, 1855.

THE STRANGE ODYSSEY OF THE GOOD SHIP LIVELY

Anderson, R., and, R. C. Anderson. *The Sailing-Ship: Six Thousand Years of History.* New York: Bonanza Books. 1963.

Barker, E. C. *The Life of Stephen F. Austin, Founder of Texas, 1793–1836.* Dallas: Cokesbury, 1926.

Brazoria County Historical Museum. Web Site, Internet.

Bugbee, L. G. "What Became of the *Lively*?" *Quarterly of the Texas State Historical Association* (October 1899): 141–47.

Fehrenbach, T. R. *Lone Star: A History of Texas and the Texans.* New York: Macmillan Publishing Company, Collier Books, 1980.

Lewis, W. S. "The Adventures of the '*Lively*' Immigrants." *Quarterly of the Texas State Historical Association* (July 1899): 1–107.

Yoakum, Esq., H. *History of Texas From Its First Settlement in 1685 to its Annexation to the United States in 1846.* Facsimile reproduction. Austin: Steck Company. 1855.

THE SPIRITS OF GOLIAD

Banks, C. S., and G. T. McMillan. *The Texas Reader.* San Antonio: Naylor, 1947.

Bigony, M. L. "In the Spirit." *Texas Parks and Wildlife Magazine* (October 1988): 2–7.

Burke, J. W. *Missions of Old Texas*. London: A. S. Barnes, 1947.

Casis, L. M., trans. "Letter of Don Damian Manzanet to Don Carlos de Siguenza Relative to the Discovery of the Bay of Espiritú Santo." *Quarterly of the Texas State Historical Association-* 2 (July 1898–April 1899): 281–312.

Chipman, D. E. *Spanish Texas*. Austin: University of Texas Press, 1992.

Coopwood, B. "Notes on the History of La Bahía del Espiritú Santo." *Quarterly of the Texas State Historical Association-* 2 (July 1898–April 1899): 162–69.

Fehrenbach, T. R. *Lone Star: A History of Texas and the Texans*. New York: Macmillan Publishing Company, Collier Books, 1980.

Lone Star Junction. Web Site, Internet.

Sowell, A. J. *Rangers and Pioneers of Texas*. Austin: State House Press, 1991.

Southwick, N. *The Evolution of a State or Recollections of Old Texas Days*. Austin: University of Texas Press, 1983.

Texas Online. Web Site, Internet.

Wheat, P. "The *Belle*: A Gift from Louis XIV." Texas Historical Commission, La Salle Shipwreck Project. Web Site, Internet.

Williams, D. S. *Ghosts Along the Texas Coast*. Plano, Tex.: Wordware Publishing, 1995.

Yoakum H. *History of Texas From Its First Settlement in 1685 to its Annexation to the United States in 1846*. Facsimile reproduction. Austin Tex.: Steck Company, 1855.

The Truth About Sasquatch

Green, J. *Sasquatch: The Apes Among Us*. Seattle: Hancock House, 1978.

Sprague, R., and G. S. Krantz. "The Scientist Looks at the Sasquatch II." *Anthropological Monographs of the University of Idaho,* no. 4. Moscow, Idaho: University Press of Idaho, 1979.

Web Sites, Internet:
American Museum of Natural History
Bigfoot Encounters
Bigfoot Researchers Organization
Global Bigfoot Encyclopedia
Hairy Hominid Archives
Internet Virtual Bigfoot Conference

Kyle's Bigfoot Web Site
Texas Parks and Wildlife

HUMMING WITH THE HUMMERS

Bierhorst, J. *The Red Swan: Myths and Tales of the American Indians.* New York: Farrar, Straus, and Giroux, 1976.

Dixon-Kennedy, M. *Native American Myth and Legend: An A–Z of People and Places.* London: Blanford, 1997.

Gates, L., and T. Gates. Hummingbird Web Site, Internet.

Hummingbird Watchers Club. Web Site, Internet.

Johnsgard, P. A. *The Hummingbirds of North America.* Washington, D.C.: Smithsonian Institution Press, 1997.

Milne, L., M. Milne, and F. Russell. *The Secret Life of Animals.* New York: Dutton, 1975.

Padden, R. C. *The Hummingbird and the Hawk: Conquest and Sovereignty in the Valley of Mexico, 1503–1541.* Columbus: Ohio State University Press, 1967.

Pollard, H. P. *Tariacuris Legacy: The Prehistoric Tarascan State.* Norman: University of Oklahoma Press, 1993.

Tyrrell, E. Q. *Hummingbirds: Their Life and Behavior.* New York: Crown Publishers, 1985.

Westwood, J. *The Atlas of Mysterious Places.* New York: Weidenfeld and Nicholson, 1987.

THAT NIGHT AT THE VAUDEVILLE

Adams, P. "The Unsolved Murder of Ben Thompson: Pistoleer Extraordinary." *Southwestern Historical Quarterly* (January 1945): 321–29.

Davis, J. L. *San Antonio: A Historical Portrait.* Austin: Encino Press, 1978.

Fisher, O. C. "The Life and Times of King Fisher." *Southwestern Historical Quarterly* (October 1960): 233–47.

Fisher, O. C., and J. C. Dykes. *King Fisher: His Life and Times.* Norman: University of Oklahoma Press, 1966.

Horan, J. D. *The Authentic Wild West: The Gunfighters.* New York: Crown Publishers, 1976.

Humphrey, D. C. *Austin: A History of the Capital City.* Austin: Texas State Historical Association, 1997.

Linsford, J. R. "How Ben Thompson Died With His Boots On." *Frontier Times* (December 1931): 81–85.

Streeter, F. B. *Ben Thompson: Man With a Gun.* New York: Fredrick Fell, 1957.